TIPU SULTAN

THE TYRANT OF MYSORE

by
Sandeep Balakrishna

Foreword by
Shatavadhani Dr. R. Ganesh

RARE PUBLICATIONS
Chennai

Total Pages : xii + 212 = 224
First Published : 2013 ISBN :
978-81-927884-6-3

Published by

Rare Books

RARE PUBLICATIONS

'Sree Vijayam"
No.9, Vijayaraghava Road, T. Nagar,
Chennai – 600 017.

E-Mail : info@rarebooksonweb.com
Website : www.rarebooksonweb.com

Printed in India at
Jayaa Prints, Chennai
Email: jayaaprints@gmail.com

Foreword

We have seen, read, and heard about a lot of phony people claiming to be freedom fighters and receiving pensions from the Government. Several of these worthies would not have been born before Independence; yet they succeed in such blatant manipulations. One portion of this unholy cesspool includes "freedom fighters," who have brutally massacred our own people, destroyed our own culture, and yet are recognized as the pioneers of our freedom struggle! Tipu Sultan happens to be one such infamous name that belongs to this cesspool. And a special brand of Indian secularism continues to render many services to perpetuate his name and fame as a freedom fighter.

Here's a small sample which can often be seen in many of the nooks and corners of Karnataka: hoardings that advertise the cause of the downtrodden, the marginalized and the suppressed by displaying the images of Buddha, Basavanna, Chennamma, Gandhi, and Tipu Sultan. I fail to understand even one aspect that's common between Buddha and Tipu. The former renounced his wealth, position and prosperity forever, lived and taught an elevated path of truth and peace and endeared himself to the entire society while the latter stood for the exact opposite. Yet, our brand of secularism finds many glowing parallels between the two.

In this chaotic state of affairs, my good friend Sandeep Balakrishna has made a bold and serious attempt in unveiling the true colours of Tipu, the "freedom fighter."

During the Nehru era, India witnessed several catastrophic changes as a result of which many new icons and ideologies were propagated and their tentacles spread far and wide and even today, the people of India continue to suffer their ill-effects. Tipu is one such heavily-eulogised icon in both our textbooks and popular media. Nowadays, our pseudo-intellectual community seems to be hell-bent upon justifying even the vilest deed committed by him. Here are just three key samples of this intellectual charlatanism:

Tipu was a great lover of books and had a wonderful library—In which case, one fails to understand why he gave away all the valuable collection of books in the royal library of Mysore to his stable to be used as fuel for cooking horse gram.

Tipu was a sensitive secularist and patronized many scholars of Hinduism including temples and mutts: Then what explains the fact that Pradhani Venkappayya (or Venkamatya), an accomplished scholar, a polymath and polyglot well-versed in the nuances of polity was imprisoned for no reason and humiliated and tortured to death?

Tipu had a scientific bent of mind and in his farsighted-ness, made many innovations in civil and military engineer-ing—In which case we don't really have a logically tenable explanation for his religious bigotry, which made him twist everything that he came across to conform to the ideology of Islam?

We have several irreconcilable facts similar to these, drawn from the murky waters of modern secularism in which our blissful intellectuals are fishing.

Although Sandeep is not the first writer to unveil these lies about Tipu, he has done a very commendable job through his comprehensive and well-documented work, which is equally readable by both the scholar and the lay person alike. His objective of providing a reliable historical account of Tipu based on primary sources after thoroughly scrutinizing them in the light of irrefutable logic has been achieved to a great extent as every chapter in the book is self-contained and well-connected to the overall narrative.

For the first time, Sandeep has consolidated many layers of historical accounts and scholarly discourses starting from contemporary British writing about Tipu to the present day debates done by the honest historians and intellectuals of India in general and Karnataka in particular. The opening chapter itself stands as a telling testimony to this fact. He has not spared any aspect of Tipu Sultan and has succeeded in forcefully demolishing the myth that Tipu was a freedom fighter.

Apart from giving a historical account of Hyder Ali's ascent to power followed by Tipu's own rise and fall, Sandeep has thrown the doors wide open and revealed Tipu's religious bigotry, economic disasters, tampering of the calendar, breaking treaties, changing the names of cities and towns to suit his Islamic bias, destroying Hindu temples, forming a battalion of forcibly converted youth for Jihad against India, and similar acts of cruelty and misdemeanour.

All of this valuable information is presented in a lucid and impeccable manner so that the reader doesn't miss the wood among the trees. Such writing is a very challenging task and at the same time, is the need of the hour because today's India is almost coming to a dead end. For this reason, we need to be courageous and honest and re-examine our past and formulate our own future based on the ideals of truth and liberty. For this purpose, I am sure that this book makes a welcome addition to the host of books published by the likes of Voice of India, Aditya Prakashan and so on.

I wholeheartedly congratulate my long-standing friend Sandeep and his publishers for taking up this much-needed work. This is because many of the earlier publications on this topic, in spite of their merits, lack some qualities which are sorely expected by the Indian youth engaged in a serious study of history. Sandeep's work fills this void and stands a class apart and makes a lasting impression in the minds of the seekers of truth.

Bangalore   *Shatavadhani Dr. R. Ganesh*
11 September 2013

Preface

In November 2012, Rahman Khan, the Union Minister of Minority Affairs announced that the Moulana Azad Education Foundation under his Ministry, was setting up five universities across the country. One of them would be established at Srirangapatna and it would be named after Tipu Sultan, the 18th century Mysore ruler. While the project of setting up these universities is not objectionable, the fact that one of them would be named after Tipu once again, showed exactly everything that's wrong with Indian politics and public life.

Guess what else is named after Tipu? A Pakistani missile. This is unsurprising given that Pakistan has been consistent in naming its missiles— Ghaznavi, Ghauri, Abdali, and Babur, all names of medieval Muslim invaders who plundered India, forcibly converted hundreds of thousands of Hindus, and destroyed their ancient culture. The fact that Pakistan, an enemy nation has named its missiles in the honour of such medieval barbarians who vowed to completely Islamize India is pretty revealing.

And here we have an Indian citizen, a Central Minister no less, who wants to establish a university named after Tipu who stands shoulder-to-shoulder with the aforementioned medieval marauders. Even worse, Rahman Khan's Government brazened out the act of naming the university after Tipu with: "the life and achievements of Tipu Sultan, who was a great warrior and secular in outlook, have been wrongly interpreted." The politician who issued this ill-informed statement neither knows nor cares whether Tipu was a great warrior or whether he was secular. What he knows is the fact that this statement sends a reassuring message to the constituents of his party's Muslim vote bank.

The myth of Tipu as a great warrior, a humanist and a tolerant ruler is one of the more enduring myths that continue to float around. This myth originated with Bhagawan S Gidwani's spurious historical novel, *The Sword of Tipu Sultan,* which was made into a television serial by Sanjay Khan and aired on the state-owned channel, Doordarshan. Over the years, this myth acquired widespread currency and today, we see things like "Mysore Tiger Tipu Association," "Tipu Nagar," and "Tipu Colony" in Muslim-dominated localities in major cities and towns of Karnataka. There was also an agitation to rename the Bangalore International Airport after Tipu.

And so we need to remind ourselves again, we need to set the record on Tipu straight before we even name something in his honour. Naming things after dead people is one of the ways to preserve their deeds, their ideals, and their legacy. So what is Tipu's record on these parameters? This book is a humble endeavour to do just that—set the record straight on Tipu starting with his full name: Tipu Sultan.

It is not as if the Myth of Tipu wasn't challenged. When Sanjay Khan mooted the idea of serializing Gidwani's novel on television, the Bombay Kerala Samajam was outraged, and challenged his depiction of Tipu by filing a case in the Bombay High Court. Much later, a prolonged debate occurred in a Kannada newspaper over the life, career, and the true legacy of Tipu. And now, with Rahman Khan's proposal, the issue has come to the forefront yet again. Apart from Rahman

Khan, more recently, the Government in Tamil Nadu has recently announced the construction of a Mani Mandapam, a memorial in honour of Tipu. One wonders what the Tamil Nadu Government would say if they learned of the story of how Tipu's father Hyder Ali completely ravaged Dindigul. Sure, we can't entirely blame Tamilnadu Government. If they were aware of facts, they would not have announced the contruction.

Distortion of history is not a new phenomenon in India. It is a well-planned and meticulously executed project that began more than four decades ago. This historical distortion is more pronounced and near-comprehensive in the case of medieval Muslim rule in India where bigots and tyrants are glorified as tolerant humanists, and those who stood up and fought against these tyrants are decried as rebels. Arun Shourie's expose of this distortion in his book, *Eminent Historians; Their Technology, Their Line, Their Fraud* is a highly recommended read for anybody who wishes to understand the motivation as well as the political skullduggery that was required to carry out this deception on a national scale.

———◆◆———

This is a book of popular history meant for easy reading. It is intentionally shorn of elaborate footnotes in order to not impede the flow of the narrative. However, every fact about Tipu's personality, career, life, and the conditions of his time has been meticulously researched and is verifiable. In fact, there is an enormous corpus of primary sources about Tipu available for anybody who wishes to study them. Indeed, the amount of material available on Tipu is a history scholar's delight. It is therefore surprising that no mainstream scholar has attempted to do serious research on Tipu and bring the complete facts to light. An attempt of sorts has been made by I.M. Muthanna in his rigorously researched and comprehensive *Tipu Sultan X'Rayed*. However, the book suffers from glaring defects in terms of its structure and presentation.

In any case, almost all primary sources on Tipu go against the fiction that Tipu was a tolerant and compassionate ruler. Tipu was from beginning to end a fanatical and extremely cruel Islamic zealot and tyrant. His 17-year long career was marked by unprovoked and barbaric raids against weaker kings and his idea of improving the economy was the impoverishment of his own subjects using extortionate methods.

——◆——

The inspiration for writing this book came from Pratap Simha, the well-known Kannada journalist and my good friend who wrote a monograph on Tipu in Kannada. I have borrowed heavily from his book for the first and the last two chapters of this book. Any translation errors are mine. He was also generous enough to provide the rare images relating to Hyder Ali and Tipu Sultan that you find in this book. Thanks Pratap, I'm extremely grateful to you.

I also owe an immense debt of gratitude to the scholar, poet, polyglot, my friend, guru, and guide Shatavadhani Dr. R Ganesh for painstakingly reading through the manuscript and writing the Foreword.

Thanks are also due to Rare Publications who have helped with the publication of this book.

And finally, thanks also to all those who have requested to remain anonymous but have supported me at every step. This book wouldn't have been possible without you.

Sandeep Balakrishna

24 September 2013
Bangalore

——➤ *x* ➤——

Contents

1

Is the Character Depicted by Girish and Gidwani the Historical Tipu Sultan?

September 2006.

"Shikshan Bachaao!"

"Save Education!"

This was the title of a seminar in Bangalore. Inaugurating it was the then Higher Education Minister of Karnataka, D.H. Shankaramurthy, who issued this statement:

Tipu Sultan was a traitor to the Kannada language. Kannada, which was the administrative language of the Mysore State under the Wodeyars, was replaced by Farsi by Tipu Sultan. He was an opponent of the Kannada language. We don't need to give him a place of respect in the history of Karnataka. It's a mistake to glorify him. It is typical to glorify Akbar, Aurangzeb and Tipu as patriots in national history. Alexander and Akbar are glorified with the "the great" suffix. Respect and honour are given to those who embarked on a conquest of our nation, and to those who defeated our own people. Instead, our textbooks need to have lessons on people who made positive contributions for the nation; the lives of people like Sir M. Vishveswarayya and Maharaja Krishnaraja Wodeyar IV who developed the state must be included in our history textbooks. What is now happening is a perversion of history.

This was enough. The usual brigade of defenders of tyrants and mass-murderers in history erupted in a cacophony of insanity. This brigade comprising charlatans of various hues suddenly became fanatical Tipu-devotees. Most of them however, were petty eminences in the world of literature, who attribute worship-worthy qualities to Tipu. In the forefront was the Jnanapith Awardee #7 Girish Karnad, who posed as if he had taken a personal contract of defending Tipu, and embarked on a campaign of shrillness.

In the meantime, D.H. Shankaramurthy reaffirmed his original statement, saying he was "ready for a public debate on the subject." In its wake, on 21 September, 2006, Girish Karnad, who has written a play on Tipu Sultan, teamed up with K. Marulasiddappa and Professor B.K. Chandrashekhar, and called a joint press conference where he thundered as follows: "I am ready for a public debate with D.H. Shankaramurthy."

But then, no signs of any such debate were forthcoming.

And that was that for the moment. The tried and tested technique of spit and run and the practiced art of intellectual evasion. It is instructive to examine their record. These likeminded folks who gang up and holler from the rooftops in a unified throat and who are all over the media. Have we ever seen them engage in a public debate even *once*? It appeared as if the same phenomenon was set to repeat in 2006 as well, that they would get away once again with their spitting and running.

When Vishweshwar Bhat, editor of a top-ranking Kannada newspaper observed this, he threw his paper open for exactly this sort of public debate—a debate that discussed the truth and the myth surrounding Tipu Sultan. One of the first and most prominent respondents was the popular and highly acclaimed Kannada litterateur, Dr. S.L. Bhyrappa. His essay dated 24 September, 2006 was titled *"It is Impossible to Build Nationalism on a Foundation based on Historical Falsehoods"* revealed the true colours of Tipu. Here's what he said in that essay. [The original essay is in Kannada. Translation is by the author of this book.]

——◆—

The currently sensational news in Karnataka politics happens to be centered on Education Minister Shankaramurthy who said that Tipu Sultan was an opponent of Kannada because he replaced Kannada, the administrative language of Mysore State, with Farsi. This statement has met with expected reactions from expected quarters. These quarters have also raised a din calling for the Chief Minister to sack Shankaramurthy failing which they would begin a severe agitation. The Education Minister has further clarified that he's willing to engage in a public debate on the issue. Meanwhile, the actor, director and playwright Girish Karnad together with his associates, K.Marulasiddappa, and former Primary Education Minister, Professor B.K. Chandrashekhar called for a press conference where he has agreed for such a public debate with Shankaramurthy. This has my wholehearted support. But then, they have already passed a judgement that Shankaramurthy's statement is dangerous and damaging to the nation. My intention is not to discuss the politics surrounding this issue. I'd like to regard Karnad as a litterateur and an artist in my response that follows.

*I read his play, Tughlaq when it was first published. His craftsmanship is good. The mixture of comic—seriousness is effective. It provides immense scope for direction. It is modeled on the existential thinker-writer, Camus' **Caligula.** I thought that there was a huge gap between the historical Muhammad Bin Tughlaq and the Tughlaq, whom Karnad had glorified as an ideal in his play. Back then, I neither had the interest nor the inclination to research more on the subject.*

*After forty years, I read Karnad's **The Dreams of Tipu Sultan.** I felt that Karnad had completely whitewashed the Tipu Sultan I had read about and instead, had portrayed him as some* *kind of a valiant but tragic hero. I say this as someone hailing from the Old Mysore region, as someone who knows more about Tipu Sultan.*

In the interim, I had also observed Girish Karnad's statements, activities, and agitations, and had concluded that he was a committed Leftist. But those were his personal beliefs. I had therefore maintained a respectful distance giving credence to the fact that everybody has a right to their own beliefs and convictions. However, after I read **The Dreams of Tipu Sultan** *and* **Tughlaq** *again, I decided to research in depth about these two historical characters to understand Girish Karnad's affinity to historical truths. History has always been one of the areas of my interest. Specifically, I've researched Indian history to an extent.*

The blurb of **Tughlaq** *explicitly states that although the plot of the play is historical, its intent is not to portray history. However, wherever this play has been staged, both the audience and the performers have invariably felt that the Tughlaq of Karnad's play was the real, historical Tughlaq. 'A Brahmin was wronged by my officers. You all have seen that I am committed to erasing this injustice and that I'm devoted to walk in the path of justice. This is an unforgettable moment in the history of our kingdom, a kingdom which is splintered due to religious strife. I want equality in my kingdom. I want progress. I want justice that is based on logic. It is not merely enough to have peace; I want the spark of life.' 'The most important fact is that Daulatabad is a city where the majority is Hindus. I want to shift my capital to Daulatabad in order to foster greater harmony between Hindus and Muslims.' Thus goes the Sultan's words. Further, the statement that 'the Sultan lapses into ecstasy whenever he witnesses the sight of a Brahmin who is with a Muslim friend' is intended to evoke a feeling in the audience that Tughlaq was far more tolerant and religiously fair minded than Akbar whom he preceded by about 230 years. But then as per Ibn Battuta, this is the same Sultan who renamed Devagiri to Daulatabad. This is the same Sultan who imprisoned and forcibly* *converted to Islam, the 11 sons of the southern king of Kampili who rebelled against him* **(Ibn Battuta, The Rehla of Ibn Battuta, Eng translation by Dr. Mahdi Hussain, 1953, pg 95. Ishwari Prasad's Qaaunah Turks in India, Vol 1, Allahabad 1936, Pg 65-66. Mahdi Hussain, Tughlaq Dynasty, Calcutta 1963, pg 207-208, quoted in "Muslim Slave System in Medieval India" by K.S. Lal, Aditya Prakashan, New Delhi, 1994).** *This same Tughlaq didn't refrain from demolishing Hindu temples and building mosques on the same spot. A mosque named Bodhan Deval exists in the Nizamabad district in Andhra Pradesh. As the name itself suggests, this is a mosque built after demolishing a preexisting temple on the site. Two inscriptions—that are still available—state that this mosque was built during the reign of Muhammad Bin Tughlaq. G.Yazdani, author of* **Epigraphia Indo-Moslemica 1919-20,** *states on page 16 that "as the name itself suggests, the Deval mosque was a Jain temple, which was converted to a mosque when Muhammad Bin Tughlaq became victorious in his raid of the Deccan." The original temple's architecture was star-shaped. However, the Muslims (Tughlaq) replaced the sanctum sanctorum with a pulpit. This apart, the temple was not significantly modified. The original pillars remain intact till date. The carvings of the Tirthankaras on the pillars too, remain intact till date* **(Sitaram Goel, Hindu Temples What happened to them? Vol II, page 67).**

According to Abu Nassir Aissi, Sultan Muhammad Bin Tughlaq planted the flag of Islam in corners that had never been conquered before, and had the verses of the Quran recited in places that had never heard them recited before. He put an end to the fire-worshipping verses and replaced them with the verses of the Azaan **(S.A.A Rizvi, India in Tughlaq's Time, Aligarh, 1956, Vol I, pg 325).** *What basis does the playwright have to depict this Sultan as tolerant, other than that of the Marxist propaganda?*

Sultan Muhammad Bin Tughlaq's exploits in slave-taking was infamous even in faraway lands. Shihabuddin Ahamad Abbas notes the Sultan's enthusiasm in this regard as follows: "the Sultan's ardour in waging war against Kashmir was unabated. The number of prisoners that he took was so staggering that everyday, thousands of slaves were sold at abysmal prices (**Masalik-ul-abisar fi Mumalik-ul-amsar. Translated in E.D. 111 Pg 580, S.A.A Rizvi, India in Tughlaq's Time**). *And it was not just in war. Tughlaq had a fancy for buying and collecting a huge number of foreign and Indian slaves. In every war or an expedition to put down rebels, the number of Kafir female-slaves that the Sultan rounded up was so huge that, as Ibn Battuta writes, "on occasion, a large number of female prisoners were rounded up in Delhi. The Nazir sent me ten of them. Of them, I returned one to the person who brought them to me. But he was not satisfied. My companion took three small girls. I don't know what happened to the rest of them* (**Ibn Batutta, ibid**).

What sort of an ideal do we think Sultan Muhammad Bin Tughlaq pursued?

Girish Karnad's mind has purposefully worked in a similar fashion in **The Dreams of Tipu Sultan.**

During the Indian freedom struggle, wandering bards, minstrels, and those who sang lavanis used to sing rustic songs that glorified Tipu at street corners, in marketplaces, and fairs. These semi-literate and illiterate people had no knowledge of history. They were patronized by Muslims, especially Muslim merchants and businessmen who gave them bakshish. In the same vein, some playwrights wrote plays glorifying Tipu as a great patriot based on the sole fact that he had fought against the British. Thus informed, the audience and general public began to believe that this was the true picture of the historical Tipu Sultan. Post-independence, our Marxists, vote bank politicians, and religiously-driven Muslim writers, artists, playwrights, and filmmakers portrayed Tipu as a patriot and a national hero. Real history died. The British were depicted as heartless villains for taking two sons of Tipu as hostages.

Girish Karnad, who adheres to this tradition of painting Tipu as a national hero takes up this hostage episode in his play and makes Tipu mouth this highly revelatory dialogue of sociology: "A new language has come to our land. A new culture. Angreji! A culture that takes children aged seven—eight as war hostages."

However, taking war hostages was a tradition practiced by Muslim rulers who ruled India. Either Girish Karnad is ignorant of the fact that the British merely followed this existing tradition or he has deliberately suppressed it. Mir Jumla, a general under Aurangzeb defeated and looted the entire treasury of the king of Assam. And he didn't stop there. He demanded more money and took the king's sons and a daughter as ransom till the king brought him the money. Mir Jumla also took the sons of the king's feudatories, Burha Go Hen, Baar Go Hen, Gad Gonia Pukhan, and Bad Patra Pukhan as war hostages. This fact is recorded by Saqi Mustad Khan in ***Masir-i-Alamgiri****, which is Aurangzeb's authorized biography (5th Al Hijra 1072, which corresponds to 5 January, 1663). During the Mughal rule, every Rajput king had to station at least one son in the Badshah's court as a sign of respect. The undertone of this arrangement was clear to both parties—the son was a glorified hostage ensuring obedience from Rajput kings. This custom was inaugurated by Akbar and continued thereafter. A Rajput ruler defeated in war had to marry his daughter off to the Mughal king—a wife but nevertheless a permanent hostage. Most Rajput kings agreed to this because of their vanquished status. Maharana Pratap was the lone exception. He refused to send his son to Akbar's court. When Khurram, who later styled himself as Shahjahan, rebelled against his own father and failed, the father Jahangir, took his son's sons—his own grandsons—Dara and Aurangzeb as war hostages. But Cornwallis who took Tipu's sons as hostages treated the boys with the care and propriety that befitted royal heirs, something that none of the Muslim rulers did under similar circumstances. If Muslim war hostages were non-Muslim, they were compulsorily converted to Islam.*

Now, what was the condition laid down for taking Tipu's sons as hostages? After he was defeated in the war, Tipu agreed to pay a certain sum of money to the British according to the terms of surrender. But his treasury was nearly empty. Neither did he have anything he could pledge until he could obtain the money. However, could the British merely believe his verbal promise? The British didn't originally intend to take the young boys as hostages. And once throughout the time they held the boys hostages, they were treated with care and courtesy.

The fact that some politicians in their speeches, praise Tipu as the "son of Kannada" is nothing new. Kannada was the official language of the state when the Wodeyar dynasty ruled the Mysore kingdom. However, Tipu replaced it with Farsi. However, as someone who hereditarily hails from a family of village accountants that reported to the Old Mysore State's Revenue department, I am well-versed with the tax paperwork. Thus, Farsi administrative terms like "Khata," "Khirdi," "Pahani," "Khanisumari," "Gudasta," "Takhte," "Tari," "Khushki," "Bagaaytu," "Banjaru," "Jamabandi," "Ahalvalu," "Khavand," "Amaldaar," and "Shirastedaar" that are still in vogue were introduced during Tipu's time.

Tipu also changed the original names of entire cities and towns: Brahmapuri became Sultanpet, Kallikote became Farookabad, Chitradurga became Farook yab Hissar, Coorg became Zafarabad, Devanahalli became Yusufabad, Dindigal became Khaleelabad, Gutti became Faiz Hissar, Krishnagiri became Phalk-il-azam, Mysore became Nazarabad (today's Nazarbad is the name of a locality in Mysore city), Penukonda became Fakrabad, Sankridurga became Muzaffarabad, Sira became Rustumabad, and Sakleshpur became Manjarabad.

Does all this reflect Tipu's nationalism, his religious tolerance, and his love for the Kannada language?

Girish Karnad has taken the title of his play, "**The dreams of Tipu Sultan**" from a collection of leaflets written by Tipu in his *own handwriting in Farsi. Major Beatson, a Britisher who edited the English edition of this collection gave it the name "**The dreams of Tipu Sultan.**" I have read this work.*

Tipu used to be anxious about the fact that he had to have absolute privacy when he was writing this, and later, while reading it. This collection was found in the royal latrine in the Srirangapattanam palace. Tipu's most loyal servant, Habibulla identified and confirmed that these were indeed written by his master. Today, both the original and the translation are at the India Office in London.

When one reads it, the true extent of Tipu's religious fanaticism becomes clearer. He always refers to Hindus as Kaffirs and the British as Christians. A long-bearded Maulvi frequently appears in his dreams; Tipu goes to Mecca on a pilgrimage; Prophet Mohammad tells a long-bearded Arab, "Tell Tipu that I shall not enter Heaven without Tipu;" Tipu is then on a mission to convert all non-Muslims to Islam and Islamizes all non-Islamic nations. Tipu never talks about modernizing India and is furious that the Christians (British) are the biggest obstacles in his path; he desires to drive them out.

Tipu, who embarked on a long campaign of the Malabar and Coorg and left a brutal trail of forcible conversion of Hindus in its wake, refrained from trying a similar stunt in the Mysore region. He needed the support of Hindus after his financial humiliation in the Third Mysore War of 1791, which was when he had to submit his two sons to the British apart from surrendering a large portion of his empire. Therefore, in a move to placate Hindus, he gave a large donation to the Sringeri Shankaracharya Mutt. Our secular-progressives project this incident as an instance of Tipu's non-sectarianism and religious tolerance.

Tipu actually wrote to the Afghan king Jaman Shah and the Caliph of Turkey to invade India and establish the rule of Islam. In his infamous sack of the Mysore palace in 1796, he rounded up the entire palace library containing invaluable ancient Hindu palm-leaf manuscripts, inscriptions, papers, and books, and ordered them to be burnt as fuel to boil gram, which was then used to feed horses.

The Muslims in the Malabar speak, read and write Malayalam even today. The same applies to Muslims in Tamil Nadu. However, Muslims in Karnataka speak only Urdu and have remained distant from mainstream Kannada. This is the direct result of Tipu's imposition of Farsi and Urdu as the only permitted mediums of instruction.

My fundamental question concerns the freedom that a novelist can assume in depicting historical persons as characters in a work of fiction based on history. A novelist definitely has absolute freedom to portray imaginary characters according to his/her wish. This is because it is the author's original creation. However, while portraying the character of an historical person, the author must adhere to historical truths. There are those argue that there is nothing like a universally agreed-upon historical truth, and that a historical truth depends on how a particular historian interprets it. If a litterateur is bound by an ideology or is directed by an ideological group, he/she will also be inevitably bound to portray every episode of history and every historical character according to the directions of that ideology or group.

Whatever maybe their internal denominations and categories— Communists, the J.N.U group, the Left—it is undeniable that Girish Karnad is an adherent of Marxism. One of the core beliefs of this group is that Islam has socialism while Hinduism doesn't. In the Cold War period, Stalin, in a bid to befriend the Arab nations to act as a bulwark against Capitalist America, reemphasized how Islam is a system that provides perfect social justice. This made it impossible for Indian Marxists, who had sold their brains to Soviet Russia, to critically examine prominent historical Muslim figures of India. Added to this was their design to instigate Muslims in the garb of supporting them in a ploy to contain the BJP, which rose to prominence on the plank of pro-Hindu causes. *Therefore, intellectuals like Karnad are always ready to stir up noises against the BJP. Be it an issue like the Datta Jayanti, or the Saraswati Vandana in schools, he is just waiting around the corner. With this level of ideological commitment, he will use his creativity in the service of ideology. Art then becomes a mere instrument of furthering his political beliefs. A litterateur must be politically neutral. Although it is extremely difficult, my personal belief is that if a litterateur enters politics, he/she must not let it influence his/her literature. However, Leftists claim that no art, ethics, economics, history and spirituality is bereft of a political dimension.*

The purpose of my essay is not to support Shankaramurthy. Neither is it to condemn historical Muslim personalities. All Muslims in India are our brothers. Our nationalism must grow stronger on the edifice of precisely this brotherhood. However, we cannot strengthen nationalism on the foundation of a false history. Almost a century has passed since we have fearlessly written about and discussed the drawbacks of Hindu society, and initiated reforms accordingly. A society becomes stronger by such candid and honest criticism and analysis. Writing the truth about the history of Muslim rule in India doesn't mean we are insulting Muslims. All of us need to learn lessons from history. If we are afraid to write the facts of history because it might offend people, if we bury the truth thus and build a false narrative of history, we cannot construct a strong building on such a false foundation. It is a sign of immaturity to blame the present generation for the mistakes committed by previous generations. Equally, it is as much a sign of immaturity for the present generation to equate itself with and project itself as the inheritors of previous generations.

───◆◆───

This devastating unmasking of Tipu by Dr. Bhyrappa was in a way, an open challenge to Girish Karnad who was forced to respond because a non-response would mean that his scholarship would stand exposed. Besides, it was Karnad who had first issued the challenge to an open debate. Thus not responding was *not* an option. And so, Karnad, who got caught in a trap of his own making, took four days before penning his response, which was published on 18 September. Just the first two paragraphs of his 19-paragraph long response are sufficient to show the true colour of both Tipu and Karnad. [Original essay in Kannada by Girish Karnad. Translation is by the author of this book.]

◆━━◆

Everybody must definitely nod their head in appreciation at the list of books Dr. Bhyrappa has read in order to write not just about Tipu Sultan, but Muhammad Tughlaq, too. He has really worked hard. However, instead of going to such pains, he should have asked me directly, I would have told him: I don't have an iota of interest in the historical Muhammad Tughlaq. I have no interest as to whether he was good or evil, whether he was pro or anti-Hindu. I wished to write an entertaining play, and in the endeavor, wanted to choose a fairly complex character. Tughlaq's life provided me that material. I took as much I wanted and used it in the manner I wanted to use.

My Tughlaq is not the historical Tughlaq. It is an imaginary character. If I wanted to write history, I would've written history instead, and not a play.

◆━━◆

Girish Karnad uses the rest of the 17 paragraphs to excoriate Bhyrappa, and to detect phony and imaginary flaws in Bhyrappa's novels. In the process, he also exposes himself as an escapist. When he says that he *"wished to write an entertaining play, and in the endeavor, wanted to choose a fairly complex character. Tughlaq's life provided me that material. I took as much I wanted and used it in the manner I wanted to use,"* it is simply a solid illustration of the exact nature of Karnad's fidelity to truth. Additionally, when he says that his

"Tughlaq is not the historical Tughlaq. It is an imaginary character. If I wanted to write history, I would've written history instead, and not a play," isn't it clear that the Tipu he created too, is imaginary? In case his Tipu was the *real,* historical Tipu, isn't the onus on Girish Karnad to prove that Tipu was not anti-Kannada and anti-Hindu? Why did he waste 17 paragraphs in a lengthy exercise of evasiveness and personal attack against Dr. Bhyrappa? What was the necessity for Karnad to self-righteously claim that he was ready for an open debate when Shankaramurthy told the truth about Tipu? Besides, wasn't his Tipu, like his Tughlaq, an imaginary character, which he used as he wanted? What then was Girish Karnad's problem?

However, Dr. Bhyrappa didn't spare this evasiveness either.

During the course of the debate in Vishweshwar Bhat's paper, Shatavadhani Dr. R Ganesh in his essay on the subject said that "truth, not logic, is the cornerstone of history." Dr. Bhyrappa echoed this in his 8 October 2008 closing essay on the Tipu debate, *"If a historian, like a novelist, seeks comfort, what is the fate of the truth?"*

——◆——

I am indebted to Sri Girish Karnad, Sumateendra Nadig, Dr. Chidananda Murthy, Dr. Suryanath Kamat, Dr. S. Shettar, Shatavadhani R.Ganesh, readers of the public who wrote their views to the paper's editor and to the editor of Vijaya Karnataka for offering a platform for free and frank discussion on the subject of my essay of 24 September entitled "It is Impossible to Build Nationalism on a Foundation based on Historical Falsehoods." It is a welcome sign that Kannada readers are so vigilant.

To continue the discussion about Muhammad bin Tughlaq and Tipu Sultan would simply mean piling facts and details. What we instead need to analyze is the political perspective from which history is being taught. I shall first recount my firsthand experience of the nature of the grip of this politics.

Around 1969-70, the Central Government under Smt Indira Gandhi mooted a programme whose aim was to foster national integration through education. To this end, it formed a committee headed by G. Parthasarathy, a former ambassador and someone who was close to the Nehru-Gandhi family. Then, I was serving as a lecturer of philosophy in the National Council of Educational Research and Training (NCERT) in Delhi, and was selected as one of the five members of this committee. During the inaugural meeting, Mr. Parthasarathy, in the smooth tone of a practiced politician spoke about the aims of the committee, "It is our duty not to sow seeds of thorns in the minds of growing children, which would in future prove to be a hurdle in national integration. Most of our history textbooks contain such seeds of thorns. These seeds are also present here and there in subjects like language and social studies. Our history and other subjects must contain lessons that foster national integration. This committee has been entrusted with such a serious responsibility."

The remaining four members respectfully nodded their heads in agreement.

I asked: "Sir, I didn't understand you. Can you please explain with examples?"

"Ghazni Mahmud broke the Somanath temple and looted it; Aurangzeb demolished the Kashi and Mathura temples and built mosques in their place, and imposed Jaziya...what purpose does these kinds of useless episodes serve in the present time other than sowing seeds of hatred? How will they help in building a strong India of the future?"

"In that case, aren't these episodes historical truths?"

"There are several truths. However, maturity and discrimination lies in using discretion in selecting them."

The rest again nodded their heads in agreement.

14

"*You gave the examples of Kashi and Mathura. Even today, lakhs of people from various corners of the country visit them each year. All of them can see with their own eyes the sight of enormous mosques, which have been built using the pillars and walls of their sacred temples, which were demolished. They can also see that the original temples—on whose site these mosques now stand—were built recently in a space as big as a cowshed. These pilgrims experience hurt when they witness this sight. When they return home, they describe this sight to their family, neighbours, friends and relatives. Does this fact help in ensuring national integration? We can suppress history in textbooks prescribed for schoolchildren. But how can we suppress it when they go on educational or other tours? Research shows us that over thirty thousand temples were demolished. Can we suppress all of them...*"

Mr. Parthasarathy cut me off and said, "*You a lecturer of philosophy. Please tell us what is the purpose of history.*"

"*Nobody can say what the purpose of history is. Nobody can predict the direction in which science and technology will take us. Some Western thinkers have written about the Philosophy of History. However, most of this kind of writing is dense. What we need to discuss here is: **what is the purpose of teaching history?** History is our quest of the truth about our past and the lives of the people of our past. It is a quest which is undertaken using instruments such as inscriptions, records, literary works, remnants, and ruins. Historical truth helps us learn lessons of not making the same mistakes our ancestors did and of imbibing their good qualities...*"

He interrupted me with, "*does that mean we can hurt the sentiments of the minorities? Can we cleave the society? Sowing poisonous seeds in the minds of children...*"

"*Sir, the very categorization as minority and majority in itself shows that there is intent to divide the society. The concept of 'poisonous seeds' contains prejudice. Why should minorities identify a sense of solidarity between themselves and Ghazni Mahmud and*

Aurangzeb? Aurangzeb's extreme narrow-mindedness in religious matters caused the Mughal Empire to disintegrate. Akbar's broad policy of religious toleration helped the Mughal Empire flourish. Can't we teach these lessons to children without betraying the historical truth? Before we teach the lessons we must learn from history, shouldn't we teach the actual historical truths? All idealistic pronouncements that cloak the truth are politically motivated. These pronouncements won't last long. Be it minorities or the majority, unless they develop the intellectual and emotional maturity that comes from facing the truth directly, any education is useless—and dangerous, even."

Mr. Parthasarathy nodded. He praised my scholarship and intellectual abilities. During lunch break, he took me to his room separately, placed his hand on my shoulder in a gesture of intimacy, and enquired about my native place. He spoke two sentences in Tamil, which contained one Kannada word, and then said that we were from neighbouring states, and that we spoke brother-languages. And then, "your points are valid academically. Write a paper on this topic. But then, when the Government makes a policy that is applicable nationally, it needs to achieve a balance between several competing interests. Pure philosophical aspects don't figure in there," he said with a triumphant smile.

When the Committee met the next day, I continued to hold my position firmly. I argued that history that wasn't based on the truth was futile and dangerous. Mr. Parthasarathy's face showed displeasure. I didn't budge. The morning session concluded without reaching any decision. Mr. Parthasarathy didn't speak to me after that. The Committee met 15 days later. My name wasn't included in it. The reconstituted Committee had replaced my name with Arjun Dev, a history lecturer committed to the Marxist ideology. All history and Social Science textbooks that the NCERT produced thenceforth were done so under his direction. These books became textbooks—or became guides to prepare textbooks—in all states ruled by the Congress or the Communist party.

Two NCERT textbooks serve as good examples to expose the design of this Marxist group to assault the minds of growing and impressionable children. Both were written by Marxist historians and prescribed as Class XI textbooks. The first is **Ancient India** by R.S. Sharma, and the other is **Medieval India** by Satish Chandra.

According to them, Ashoka's policy of religious toleration included extending respect even to Brahmins. Because Ashoka had prohibited the slaughter of animals and birds, the livelihood of Brahmins, which depended on the dakshina they received for conducting Homas and Havans, was threatened. After Ashoka, Brahmins ruled over several parts of the splintered Mauryan Empire. This immature reasoning extends even to the temples that were destroyed by Muslim invaders. The reasoning given is that temples were destroyed because the Muslim invaders wanted to loot the enormous wealth they contained! In other cases, it says that temple destructions occurred because of the Sharia law. However, Dr. B.R. Ambedkar in **the Decline and Fall of Buddhism (Writings and Speeches, Volume III, Government of Maharashtra, 1987 PP229-38)** narrates how Muslim raiders razed to the ground the great Buddhist universities of Nalanda, Vikramashila, Jagaddala, Odantapuri, etc, and committed the genocide of hundreds of thousands of Buddhist monks. Those who managed to escape this mass murder fled to Nepal and Tibet. Dr. Ambedkar then remarks, "The axe fell upon the roots of Buddhism. By killing the priestly class of the Buddhists, Islam killed Buddhism itself. This is the most brutal calamity visited upon Buddhism in India."

When it suits their Hindu-baiting purposes, these Marxists selectively quote Dr. Ambedkar. However, they actively suppress the same Ambedkar—who fought against the Hindu Varna system and became a Buddhist towards the end of his life—who says that Muslims were responsible for the brutal destruction of Buddhism in India.

*R.S. Sharma, in **Ancient India, New Delhi, 1992 Pg 11** writes: "The enormous wealth of the Buddhist viharas attracted the Turkish raiders. They were special targets for the greed of these raiders. The Turks killed numerous Buddhist monks. Despite this, several of them escaped to Nepal and Tibet."*

The clever Marxists have tried to suppress a crucial fact here. By calling them Turks (a tribal name), they have tried to conceal the fact that these raiders were Muslims and that they destroyed the viharas motivated by their religion's strictures. However, they also write that Buddhism in Ashoka's time was destroyed by Brahmins who coveted dakshina. We do need to appreciate the shrewdness of these worthies who suppress the truth and create falsehood at the same time.

Western historians who began to write India's history by following the European historical method have paved us a good path. But their scholarship was fuelled by an ulterior motive. They had already developed the following narrative: Indian culture is the Vedic culture. The creators of this culture were Aryans, who came into India from abroad. They destroyed the native culture and established themselves here. Thus, everybody who came thereafter were alien invaders. At one stage the Muslims came. Now, the British have come. Therefore, if somebody argued that the British weren't native to India, they had a readymade response: neither are you. This was institutionalized in universities, and the media. English-educated young men and women carried this perception, too. This narrative also informed that the Rg Veda, held sacred by the Aryans was composed by them when they were outside India. This narrative severed the spiritual bond that connected Indians with India. The result was that over hundred years, English-educated Indians suffered a sense of alienation. This narrative also germinated and escalated the discord among some Indians who saw themselves as the native Dravidians whom the invading Aryans subjugated. Those who understand human nature well know that it is easy to beget enmity and that when it is proved that the enmity is based on false reasons, it is still difficult to let go of ill-feeling.

The Aryan Invasion Theory was disproved eventually by several researches, which showed plenty of evidence against the occurrence of such an invasion. However, nobody had written a comprehensive work on Indian history from the Indian perspective. In this backdrop, the freedom fighter, Gandhian, distinguished lawyer, member of the Constituent Assembly, eminent scholar, and founder of the Bharatiya Vidya Bhavan, Kanhaiyalal Munshi conceived of a project to write a comprehensive history of India. He invited the towering History scholar and researcher, R.C. Majumdar to become the editor. The two entered into an agreement. It was Munshi's responsibility to provide equipment and money that Majumdar asked for. Additionally, Munshi would have **no** say in the selection of scholars (who would be invited to write on specific areas of history) and other editorial tasks. Munshi honoured this agreement. Thus came to be written the **History and Culture of the Indian People** in 11 volumes written by scholars who were specialists in various themes and sub-themes of history. No other work in comparable scope or depth or fidelity to truth has been attempted either singly or jointly in the last fifty years. I had read all the volumes. If one reads a specific section or period as it is classified in these volumes, it provides the complete and up-to-date research done on it including references to primary sources. All that remains is adding contemporary research—if any—and republishing a new edition. My personal collection contains all these 11 volumes.

The National Book Trust put out a proposal to translate these 11 volumes into all Indian languages. The proposal was forwarded to the Indian Council for Historical Research (ICHR) because it pertained to history. The ICHR formed a Committee to examine the proposal. The Committee was headed by S.Gopal and included Tapan Roy Choudhury, Satish Chandra and Romila Thapar. By then, the ICHR was completely under the control of Marxists. Expectedly, they recommended that the Bharatiya Vidya Bhavan volumes were unsuitable for translation into Indian languages and that the proposal should not be carried forward. And it didn't stop *at just that. It suggested an alternative works that had potential for such a translation. These alternative works were authored by the selfsame Committee members and their other Marxist comrades. Five books authored by the Chairman of ICHR, R. S.Sharma, three books by S. Gopal (son of the renowned scholar and philosopher, S.Radhakrishnan), three by Romila Thapar, two by Bipan Chandra, two by Irfan Habib, two by his father Mohammad Habib, one by Satish Chandra, works of the Communist Party of India's leading light, E.M.S Namboodiripad, and one book by Rajni Palme Dutt, who was guiding and controlling the Indian Communists in the 1940s. Not a single book by Lokamanya Tilak, Jadunath Sarkar or R.C. Majumdar! (In this connection, it is worth reading Arun Shourie's Eminent Historians: Their Technology, Their Line, Their Fraud, ASA 1998. Arun Shourie is hated by different groups for different reasons. A defining characteristic of Arun Shourie's writing is the fact that it delves into the deepest roots of the issue it discusses. **Eminent Historians** provides the complete list of the remuneration that each person took for the aforementioned translation project.)*

Towards the end of his life, Gandhiji's ideas and influence had waned within the Congress party. Nehru was never a follower of Gandhiji's ideas. Although Nehru had great admiration for the British system of democracy, his heart really lay with Russia's Communism. After he became Prime Minister, he slowly sidelined most leaders within the Congress. Patel's death became a boon to Nehru. As President, Rajendra Prasad was reduced to the status of a respectable token. Although leaders like Rajagopalachari and Kriplani quit the Congress party and formed their own outfits, their influence was insignificant. Nehru, who was influenced by a hardcore Marxist like Krishna Menon wasn't naïve. Although he earned some goodwill in the international community as the leader of the Non-aligned Movement, he had to face opposition from America because the NAM was essentially sympathetic to Communist Russia. The result was India's loss. However,

*India's loss wasn't Nehru's loss. Nehru's worshipful love for the Communist ideology had reached such proportions that his Government and the Indian media routinely chanted the **Hindi-Chini bhai bhai (India-China brothers)** slogan until India was kicked out of its own territory by China. By then Marxists had occupied the intellectual space in India. For his political survival, Nehru practiced the policy of pitting Hindus against themselves and simultaneously, of appeasing Muslims. This was the tactic the British had instituted for maintaining their colonial hold over India, which Nehru continued. The word "casteism" became a term of abuse reserved only to be used against Hindus. Further, he also spread the perception that secularism was something that only Hindus needed to practice towards Muslims and Christians because being minorities, they were incapable of casteism.*

*Mohammad Karim Chagla was born, raised, and educated in Bombay. He became famous as a lawyer and earned goodwill and respect as a man of integrity. He went on to become the Chief Justice of the Bombay High Court and retired from the position. He recounts in his autobiography, **Roses in December** that he was desirous of contesting the Lok Sabha elections. He wrote to Nehru requesting him to give a ticket from a constituency in Bombay. The Congress High Command acceded to his request. In its reply, it said that he would be given a ticket to contest from the Aurangabad constituency. In turn, he replied with, "I was born, raised, and I have served the public in Bombay. People know me well here. Why have you given me a ticket in faraway Aurangabad where I know nobody and about which I know nothing?" Nehru's High Command retorted, "Aurangabad has a large Muslim population. Because you are a Muslim, you contest from there."*

I was a small boy when the country achieved freedom and held its initial general elections. However, I've witnessed Congress leaders discussing the relative strengths and reach of castes in a particular constituency, and caste-based leaders who needed to be nominated for elections.

Indira Gandhi, whose sole aim was to retain and remain in power, required the help of the Communists against her opponents that included the fast-growing Jana Sangh, and the ex-Congress combine of Morarji Desai, Nijalingappa, Neelam Sanjiva Reddy, Kamaraj and others. On their part, the Communists realized that they didn't have enough strength to capture power on their own. They reasoned that putting their ideology in positions of power was a good alternative. Indira Gandhi thus helped the Communists infiltrate key institutions like the ICHR, NCERT, universities and the media. Additionally, Communist Russia exerted external pressure to make this happen. Nehru and his daughter had by then stooped to a position of weakness, which prevented them from taking a strong stance against Russia even in key domestic matters. Once the Communists were firmly entrenched in the nation's key intellectual nerve centres, they began to shape the direction of these institutions following the model already laid down by Communist dictatorships like Russia and China. Now, Sonia Gandhi's UPA Government is anyway dependent on the life support given by the Communists (Note: this article was written in 2008, during the first innings of the UPA Government. Communist parties supported the Government from outside.).

When the Leftists began to occupy the Government's Education department, the History department, and the departments of history, sociology and literature, the media adopted a studied ignorance. When Murli Manohar Joshi, the NDA's HRD Minister began to introduce changes that emphasized Indianness in our education, these Leftists raised a shrill cry. His changes included things like teaching the contribution of ancient India to science, and beginning classes with the Saraswati Vandana. The media projected this as a major calamity. Congress party workers and social-equality champions took out rallies and raised slogans predicting doomsday for India. Now, when the UPA Government's Arjun Singh has embarked on a project of severely re-Marxifying education, none of these worthies have raised a word of protest. The media, especially the English media, has been highly supportive of this. The Congress party, whose only aim is to remain in power, has completely lost even the semblance of intellectualism. It remains in blissful slumber content and secure in the knowledge that it can borrow intellectualism from the Left if and when required. However, it has followed the policy of economic liberalization because of its realization that its past experiment with socialism brought India to the brink of bankruptcy. However, the Communists who have accepted this have been unable to break away from Marxism from which they derive their very identity.

The tactics of Marxists to capture power in all spheres and at all levels is no different from that of caste politics, which has proved to be a curse upon India. They appoint people sympathetic to their ideology in universities, infiltrate print and television media with their fellow travelers, write glowing reviews of books written by authors loyal to their ideology, sideline authors who hold opposing or alternate views, organize ideologically-motivated seminars and camps to attract young minds to their side, exert influence on the Government to give out awards to people who follow their ideology...they have done this in a systematic manner. Critiquing a literary work by using ideology as the yardstick is the method of literary criticism that Marxists introduced in India. By doing this, they feel they have destroyed traditional measures and conceptions of literary criticism such as Rasa (Feeling or Emotion), Dhwani (Suggestion), and Auchitya (Appropriateness).

Truth for the Communists is the position the Party takes. This holds true for values like art and ethics. We don't need to explain this to people who have read books published by Communist Russia on these topics and sold at dirt cheap prices.

I have always been interested in sociology, psychology, history and allied subjects in the humanities. I have done some reading in these. Philosophy is the subject of my profession. Aesthetics was the topic of my doctoral research. However, my proclivity made me turn *to writing literature, writing novels specifically. As long as I can remember, my mind has dwelled on the nature of the relationship between truth and beauty, and literature and truth. What is the nature and extent of the freedom that a writer has in recreating an actual historical character, information about whose life and times is based on literary, archeological and other evidences? This question has bothered me at every step. The preface to **The Real Tipu** written by S.D. Sharma has further intensified my thoughts: "Tipu Sultan has recently leapt from the pages of history to the television screen. This has naturally aroused curiosity about him and his times. It has also caused great controversy. This is because several—especially, people from Kerala—hold the view that the real Tipu was not the same person that is being depicted in the Doordarshan serial. The serial, based on Bhagawan S. Gidwani novel, **The Sword of Tipu Sultan** is a book filled with falsehoods. It is a narrative that wrongly portrays factual historical events. Doordarshan's serial has given us a gift that is far from the truth. This controversy made me study Tipu Sultan in detail. When I learnt the truth about him, I was aghast."*

Forget Indian cinema, especially Bollywood cinema, which sells titillating products. It is no different with those who write Lavanis. But why do those who write serious literature indulge in titillation of a different kind? Why aren't they faithful to historical truths? Why don't they escape from the clutches of historians committed to their ideology and use their independent critical faculties to study and understand historical evidence? S. Shettar (past Chairman of the ICHR) who justifies Girish Karnad says, "In his play about Tipu, Girish Karnad has kept only the play in view and has tried to explore the good qualities of Tipu. Historians, playwrights, and creative artists each have their own ideals." What are the differences between ideology and ideal here? The litterateur can somehow escape using the parachute of convenience called ideal. However, if a historian too tries to use this convenience, what will be the fate of historical truths?

Marxist historians just don't seem to understand the importance and subtlety of this question. The less said about the litterateurs who are in their clutches the better.

◄◆►

No matter how hard Girish Karnad tries to slither his way out by claiming that *"if I wanted to write history, I would've written history instead, and not a play,"* he simply cannot pass muster. One of the descriptions of Girish Karnad's play *The Dreams of Tipu Sultan,* reads as follows:

Tipuvina Kanasugalu (English: The Dreams of Tipu Sultan) is a Kannada play written by Indian playwright Girish Karnad. The play has been performed many times but different groups around the world but mostly in the subcontinent mainly in Pakistan and India. The story follows the last days as well as the historic moments in the life of the Ruler of Mysore, Tipu Sultan, through the eyes of an Indian court historian and a British Oriental scholar.

The figure of Tipu Sultan has continued to dominate Indian and British imagination for over two centuries, as the endless flow of scholarly works, ballads, plays and novels about his tempestuous life and tragic end testifies. What, however, is less well known is that this man, who spent a large part of his life on horseback, maintained a record of his dreams, which he kept concealed from his nearest associates. **The Dreams of Tipu Sultan** *examines the inner life of this warrior, political visionary, and dreamer.*

What does this mean?

Karnad who tries to defend the indefensible on the pretext of the "Tipu of my imagination" cannot escape from the fact the Tipu of his play *is* the historical Tipu. Except that he has garlanded his Tipu with a string of falsehoods. For those who have followed Girish Karnad's career, it is clear that he has been a lifelong adherent and an ardent proponent of a spurious brand of secularism specific to India, which simply means an appeasement of Muslims at all levels and in all spheres including history.

The fact that Girish Karnad will stoop to any level to appease Muslims was very evident by his behavior at the Tata Literature Live, a literary festival held in Mumbai in November 2012. He was invited to speak on his experiences in theatre. However, not only did he *not* speak on his assigned topic, he misused the dais by indulging in an unprovoked rant against V. S. Naipaul for his "antipathy towards Indian Muslims." He alleged that Naipaul received the Nobel for insulting Muslims, and that "many of us saw it as a result of his being a nice brown face spouting venom against Muslims."

What kind of integrity, honesty, and truthful history can we expect from a person with a mindset of appeasement?

◆◆

It is unfair to single out Girish Karnad for such harsh treatment for he was merely following the template set in by Bhagwan S. Gidwani whose novel *The Sword of Tipu Sultan* was published in 1976. Gidwani claims in the preface that it is a historical novel based on the life of Tipu Sultan and declares pompously that

...No one had attempted a fair portrayal of the events in [Tipu's] life and general shape of his character. Even some of the subsequent writers had been content to accept the many distortions passed to them...Someone I thought, was needed to tear away this veil of mystery. Having no one else whom I could command, I appointed myself for the task.

Not only has Gidwani *not* portrayed the true picture of Tipu, he has deliberately distorted and suppressed historical facts in his zeal to anoint Tipu a national hero, a compassionate ruler, an apostle of religious tolerance, a ruler learned in high philosophy, and a freedom fighter. The Tipu Sultan of Gidwani's creation can do no wrong and can be seen in nothing less than angelic light. Every time things go wrong, it is the fault of mostly the British, depicted as bloodthirsty marauders who take special delight in burning down entire villages and towns. And these are just the most glaring assaults that Gidwani commits on history. Indeed, we find an accurate assessment of historical authenticity in *The Sword of Tipu Sultan* in a review of the novel by M.C. Gabriel in the *Hindustan Times* dated 19 December 1976:

> *The author's effort throughout is to rebuild the past **closer to his heart's desire**. But anyone will grant that **such consideration is extra-historical....it is a pity that...he could not put his material to better purpose than giving us just his private views**...To say that Tipu was 'the first nationalist,' 'a believer in communal harmony' and an 'apostle of non-violence'....is quite uncalled for.* [Emphasis added]

Mr. Gabriel was being restrained in his criticism of Gidwani. To put it bluntly, *The Sword of Tipu Sultan* is a phony novel whose claims to historical accuracy are as true as the fire is cold. There is simply no way Gidwani could portray Tipu as he has done without falsifying history on an industrial scale.

However, *The Sword of Tipu Sultan* became a bestseller thanks mainly to the political climate of the time. In his authoritative and encyclopedic *Tipu Sultan X-rayed*, Dr. I.M. Muthanna calls Gidwani's bluff in great detail and attributes the success of the novel quite presciently:

> *Gidwani's Tipu has a political value today, especially after the Congress Government in 1974, perhaps to oblige the Muslim voters, released a commemoration stamp on Tipu, and described him as a 'freedom fighter.'...Releasing a 50-Paisa postage stamp commemorating Tipu in July 1974, a minister of Karnataka said*

that Tipu was 'a hero' of Karnataka, 'the defender of freedom,' and so on. The chariman of the stamp releasing committee...wanted the writers to 'present a true and faithful account' of Tipu. Well... Gidwani has obliged him, rather sneakily, and in the form of a novel.

We find an echo of the same cynical political phenomenon working behind the success of Girish Karnad's celebrated play, *Tughlaq.* Like Gidwani, Karnad too, has distorted history in order to depict the medieval Muslim ruler Muhammad Bin Tughlaq as a misunderstood genius ahead of his time.

Unfortunately, voices of sage reviewers like Mr. Gabriel remained in the cold. The success of Gidwani's novel ensured that Tipu's image as a national hero and freedom fighter captured both popular imagination and proved very handy for the political class. A testimony to the endurance of this myth can be found in the selfsame Girish Karnad's play, *The Dreams of Tipu Sultan,* and a recent proposal by the Government of India to name a new university after Tipu.

2

The Rise and Rise of Hyder Ali

1799, June 24.

Your having conferred on our child the government of Mysore, Nagar, and their dependencies, and appointed Purnaiya to be the Diwan, has afforded us the greatest happiness. Forty years have elapsed since our government ceased. Now you have favoured our boy with the government of this country, and nominated Purnaiya to be his Diwan. We shall, while the sun and moon continue, commit no offence against your government. We shall at all times consider ourselves as under your protection and orders.

Your having established us must forever be fresh in the memory of our posterity, from one generation to another. Our offspring can never forget an attachment to your government, on whose support we shall depend.

--Signed

Lakshmi Ammanni

Devaji Ammanni

This letter was written to the then British Government (the East India Company) by the respective widows of the Mysore Wodeyars, Chikka Krishnaraja Wodeyar and Chamaraja Wodeyar.

If Tipu Sultan is termed a freedom fighter merely because he fought the British, then it would stand to reason to call Lakshmi Ammanni and Devaji Ammanni as traitors. It would equally stand to reason to call the Diwans under the British rule as traitors. Yet when we examine the historical truths surrounding Tipu Sultan, the British, the Mysore Wodeyars, and a host of other actors during that period, a wholly different picture emerges.

To do this, we need to ask why the royal widows wrote that letter to the British to begin with.

As the letter indicates, more than 40 years had passed since the Mysore kingdom had lapsed from the hands of the Wodeyars. During that period, Mysore was ruled by Hyder Ali and his son, Tipu Sultan. Not just that. During those 40 years, this father-son duo embarked on a series of campaigns of rapine, cruelty, and in general, unleashed a frenzy of destruction in South India.

So who were Hyder Ali and Tipu Sultan and how did the throne of Mysore pass into their hands?

The Origins of Hyder Ali

When we begin to trace Hyder Ali's antecedents, we meet with several surprises. The greatest surprise perhaps is the fact that he was a mere soldier, a mercenary for hire in reality. Born in 1721, his rise in the military ranks was astonishingly swift before ultimately usurping the throne of the Wodeyars in 1761.

Yet most histories about Hyder Ali's origins are in the vein of exaggerated hagiography, which trace his origins to royalty. This is understandable because historians of the yore typically tried (and mostly succeeded) to attribute royal descent for any warrior or hero or leader who founded and built an empire and left behind an heir or dynasty. Neither is this phenomenon restricted only to India. Historians the world over have indulged in this exercise.

In Hyder Ali's case, during his own lifetime, there were widely-circulated tales about his descent from a royal

A Portrait Sketch of Hyder Ali

lineage. It was said that he descended from a class of nobility called Quereshi. According to local legend, a person named Hassan came to Ajmer from Baghdad. The progenitor of the Hassan lineage was a man named Yahya. In Ajmer, Hassan fathered a son named Wali Mohammad, who fought with his uncle and migrated to the Deccan Plateau before finally settling down in Gulbarga. Wali Mohammad's son was Ali Mohammad, who migrated to Kolar. He fathered four sons. Ali Mohammad died in 1678.

One of Ali's sons, Fateh Mohammad became a soldier. In the battle of Ganjikota, Fateh displayed extraordinary prowess. Impressed with his abilities, the Subedar of Sira bestowed the title of *Nayaka* (Leader or Hero) upon Fateh. Shortly, this Subedar was transferred. Fateh too, left the place in search of better prospects. He joined the services of the Nawab of Arcot and later, the Nawab of Chittoor. Finally, he came to the Mysore region. He was appointed as the *Faujdaar* (Military Commander) and received the Budikota jahgir as a reward for his services. He married a girl hailing from the *Sayyadaani* clan and begot three sons from her. Then he married two sisters from the Nawayati family, who belonged to the Hashim clan. The younger sister gave birth to two sons. The first was named Shahbaaz Khan, and the second, Hyder.

This in brief was the widely-circulated legend about Hyder Ali's antecedents.

However, this account has several inconsistencies. Wilks, in his work on the history of South India gives a different picture about Hyder Ali's ancestors. Accordingly, Hyder Ali's great grandfather was a poor Muslim devotee named Mohammad Bhailal. Originally from Punjab, Bhailal migrated to South India in search of employment. He arrived at Aland—then in the Hyderabad region—and settled there. His two sons, Ali Mohammad and Wali Mohammad joined as soldiers in the army of the Subedar of Sira. Subsequently, they migrated to Kolar where Ali Mohammad died. Then Fateh Mohammad and his mother were turned out of the house by Wali Mohammad, the younger brother of Ali.

Bhailal or Bilal is originally an Afghan name. However this maybe, there is unanimity in the fact that Hyder Ali's origins are shrouded in mystery. Because Hyder usurped the Mysore kingdom and appointed himself as the King, efforts were made to show that he descended from a royal or noble lineage. What is beyond doubt is the fact that he was the son of a person named Fateh Mohammad.

In order to understand how Hyder Ali came in contact with the Mysore Wodeyars, it is necessary to briefly examine the political situation of that period as well as the history of the Mysore Wodeyars.

The founder of the Mysore Wodeyar dynasty was Vijayaraja, a Paladin who originally hailed from Dwaraka in the Kathiawad region in Gujarat. He migrated southwards with his brother Krishnaraja and arrived at a province called Hadinadu near Mysore. A neighbouring chieftain abducted the princess of Hadinadu and tried to marry her forcibly. Vijayaraja intervened, defeated the chieftain, married the princess, and settled there. He was then crowned as the Wodeyar. From the start, the Wodeyars were subordinates of the all-powerful Vijayanagar Empire.

The descendants of this dynasty were powerful for about 200 years in this region. The seventh-generation king named Raja Wodeyar was reputed to be a warrior of the highest order. In about 1609, he noticed the fact that the Vijayanagar Empire had badly weakened and declared himself independent. He took over the fort of Srirangapattana and made it his capital. Raja Wodeyar is credited with expanding the dominions of the Mysore kingdom and filling its coffers.

During this period, the Mughal Empire was ruled by Shahjahan. He had appointed his youngest son, Aurangzeb as the viceroy of the Deccan. Much of South India was under the rule of the Bijapur Sultan during this period. Upon becoming the Mughal Emperor, Aurangzeb decided to crush the power of the Marathas and the Bijapur Sultan. And so, in 1687, he defeated the Bijapur Sultan and made Sira one of the administrative headquarters of the Mughal Empire. The imperial deputy at Sira reported directly to the Mughal Badshah at Delhi. However, the fate of Sira underwent a drastic change after the death of Aurangzeb.

In 1729, Sira was administered by Dargah Kuli Khan under whom Hyder Ali's father, Fateh Mohammad served. After Kuli Khan's death, his son, Abdur Rasool Khan took over as the Subedar. Shortly, the Nawab of Arcot, Sadatullah Khan attacked Sira. Fateh Mohammad, and Rasool Khan and his entire family were killed in the war. Fateh Mohammad's wife and children were also plundered and rendered homeless. In dire poverty, they left for Bangalore in search of a home and livelihood. Hyder Ali's brother, Shahbaaz joined the Mysore army as a soldier. In a short period, he became the head of a unit comprising 100 foot soldiers and 200 horsemen.

Back to the Wodeyars, the preeminent ruler in the line of successors of Raja Wodeyar was Chikka Devaraja Wodeyar (1671-1704) who was a distinguished warrior and an excellent administrator. During his rule, Aurangzeb decided to launch an attack against Mysore. In a move of superb diplomacy, Chikka Devaraja Wodeyar sent a delegation to Aurangzeb for negotiation. The negotiation was a huge success. In 1699, Aurangzeb entered into a treaty with him, and was so pleased that he conferred the title of *Jagadeva* upon Chikka Devaraja Wodeyar. He also gifted Chikka Devaraja a throne made of ivory.

However, the successors of Chikka Devaraja Wodeyar were weak. They were reduced to being puppets in the hands of ministers and *Dalawais* (Commander in Chief) who ran the show from behind the throne. When Dodda Krishnaraja Wodeyar who ruled from 1716-33 died, the dynasty was left without a direct heir. A boy named Chamaraja Wodeyar was adopted and installed on the throne. However, the actual reins were in the hands of the Dalawai. Chamaraja Wodeyar ruled for a mere three years and died in prison. After this, in 1736, Chikka Krishnaraja Wodeyar was adopted and installed on the throne.

This then was the state of affairs in Mysore.

A Hired Mercenary Gains Prominence

In 1749, the Dalawai directed the unit of Shahbaaz Khan stationed at Bangalore to launch an attack against Devanahalli. He was joined in this campaign by his younger brother, Hyder Ali. It was in this episode that Hyder's gallantry and courage drew everybody's attention. Hyder was a mere foot soldier, a volunteer serving in his brother's unit. Lewin B. Bowring in his *Haidar Ali and Tipu Sultan* describes him as "being...of irregular habits, and addicted to low pursuits, but he was a keen sportsman and full of dash and energy. He was wholly illiterate, and indeed never learned to write."

However, the one who actually recognized Hyder Ali's prowess and capabilities was the Mysore minister Nanjaraja. He promoted Hyder as the head of a small unit of troops. Hyder's gradual but certain ascent began after this promotion. He shrewdly, cynically exploited the political situation at the time and grew at an astonishing pace. This apart, the shaky politics of South India was another important reason, which helped Hyder take control of the entire administrative machinery of Mysore.

The Mughal Empire disintegrated after Aurangzeb's death in 1707. Rebellion erupted in all corners of the Empire. In South India, various ambassadors, feudatories, and governors openly defied the Mughal Emperor's authority and declared independence. In 1713, the Mughal Emperor appointed Kamaruddin Chain Khalij Khan as the viceroy of the Deccan by bestowing upon him the title of *Nizam ul Mulk*. The Pathan Nawabs of Arcot, Kadapa, Kurnool, and Savanur had to pay tribute to him. Before his death in 1748, Kamaruddin had appointed his daughter's son, Muzaffar Jung as his successor. This greatly angered Kamaruddin's own son, Nasir Jung who forcibly occupied the throne. The inevitable war broke out for the *Nizamat* (Nizam-hood) between nephew and uncle.

The Mysore Wodeyar, who was the feudatory of the Nizam, supported Nasir Jung. It was in this war that Hyder Ali, with his small unit, accompanied his elder brother against the Nawab of Arcot under the orders of the minister of Mysore.

This war proved to be a decisive turning point in Hyder's life. But first, a quick look at the political situation of South India at the time.

The British, the French, and the Dutch had already set foot in India and were vying with one another to establish commercial superiority. They were not averse to using military methods if that was what it took. Mostly, the British and the French were engaged in a war to assert supremacy over the Madras region. The Mughal Empire as we have seen was on its last legs. The Muslim Nawabs of South India didn't share a good rapport with the Nizam of the Deccan. Family members of various Muslim rulers plotted against one another to capture power.

The royal family of the Nawab of Arcot—who was appointed by the Mughals—witnessed pitched battles for

Hyder Ali's Battle with the British

power. Mohammad Said or Sadatullah Khan, who ruled as the Nawab of Arcot from 1710-32, raided Abdul Rasool Khan, the Subedar of Sira. It was in this battle that Hyder Ali's father, Fateh Mohammad perished. After Sadatullah Khan's death, his son-in-law, Dost Ali Khan became the Nawab. He embarked on a campaign against Mysore and returned after being roundly beaten by Chikka Krishnaraja Wodeyar. Dost Ali Khan's son-in-law, Hussain Dost Khan alias Chanda Sahib had treacherously defeated the king of Puducherry (Pondicherry) and occupied the throne there. He then struck a deal with the French.

Safdar Ali Khan, who became the Nawab of Arcot after Dost Ali Khan, was murdered within two years. His minor son was installed on the throne, and a guardian named Anwaruddin oversaw the administration. At a later date, Anwaruddin perished near Ambur in a battle with the French. Anwaruddin's son, Mohammad Ali entered into an alliance with the British.

The British and the French in such conditions of overwhelming political instability began to bake their own beans by entering into pacts of convenience with these Nawabs and Chieftains. This was the reason they participated in the war for the *Nizamat* that broke out between Muzaffar Jung and Nasir Jung. The British forces were led by Major Lawerence and fought on the side the Nawab of Arcot, Mohammad Ali who fought in support of Nasir Jung. On the other side, the French troops were led by Colonel De Bussy who supported Muzaffar Jung.

It was during this war that Hyder Ali led his small contingent of the Mysore army to support Nasir Jung. Nasir Jung won the first round owing partly to a mutiny that erupted among the French troops. However, within a short span of time, the French, with the help of the Nawabs of Kadapa and Kurnool, attacked Nasir Jung at Arcot. In the short battle, Nasir Jung was treacherously murdered by the Nawab of Kadapa while Mohammad Ali fled to Tiruchinapalli.

However, this war was the first turning point in Hyder Ali's life.

Hyder Ali was basically a soldier-for-hire. As such, he wasn't bound by loyalty to any side. Although he was a gallant warrior, his mental makeup was that of a bandit. Hyder's troop of highly trained and fierce soldiers that helped Nasir Jung also made the most of the episode. In the words of Lewin Bowring,

Haidar, with the mercenary instinct of a freebooter, took advantage of the confusion to seize, with the aid of his Bedar (army of people belonging to the hunter caste) followers, a large amount of the late Nizam's treasure, with which he retreated to Mysore. Before doing so, he paid a visit to Pondicherry, where he formed a high opinion of the discipline of the French troops and of the skill of their engineer officers.

The booty that he looted from the dead Nizam was the seed that spurred his ambition to greater heights.

Hyder Ali's Ascent

In 1751, Hyder Ali got an opportunity to engage in a raid. This time too, Hyder was the leader of a contingent of the Mysore army deputed to march against Tiruchinapalli. Muhammad Ali who had fled to Tiruchinapalli requested the support of the Mysore Dalwai in a war against the French. In return, he would cede Tiruchinapalli and all the territory south of it to Mysore. The war lasted for about four years. Nanjaraja, the minister of Mysore had spent an enormous sum of money on this battle. Both the French and the English participated in this war. However, thanks to Muhammad Ali's treachery, the Mysore army was unable to obtain Tiruchinapalli. And so it withdrew its troops in 1755.

However, Hyder Ali personally profited in this war as well. In the battles that took place at Pudukottai, which is located between Tanjavur and Tiruchinapally, Hyder Ali managed to capture a sizeable number of guns of a British convoy which was separated from the main unit. Using a portion of the wealth that he had looted from the Nizam's treasury earlier, he managed to expand his army of hunters. His private unit now comprised a highly-trained force of about 1500 horsemen and 3000 infantry apart from lesser-trained troops. Again, his eye was on achieving his long-term ambition. To quote Bowring,

To assist [Hyder] in organizing the system of plundering, which he carried on for many years, he took into his service a Maratha Brahman named Khande Rao, whose literary qualifications made amends for his own want of education. But although compelled to have recourse to this extraneous aid, Haidar had a most retentive memory, which, added to his acute penetration, made it very difficult to deceive him.

He expanded this force by recruiting thousands of untrained fighters and warriors additionally.

In the same year, 1755, he was promoted to the position of a *Faujdaar* (Military Commander) at Dindigul. Hyder Ali, whose position till then was slightly better than that of a mere solider-for-hire, suddenly acquired a new, official respectability. This enabled him to launch successive and profitable raids against tiny principalities, which in turn helped him amass a massive booty. He used this money to expand his army and arsenal. By then the size of his army had swelled to about 5000. He also sought the help of the French army engineers stationed in Puducherry. These further strengthened the foundations of his long-term ambitions.

The Maratha expedition to the South came as a boon to Hyder Ali who was stationed at Dindigul. The Tiruchinapalli war, which had caused massive losses to the Mysore army, was followed by another ominous portent. Salabat Jung had taken over as the new Nizam with the help of the French Colonel De Bussy. In an ambitious expedition, he teamed up with the French and laid siege to the fort of Srirangapattana and demanded a huge tribute from the Wodeyar who was only ruling nominally. The distraught and near-bankrupt state of Mysore somehow managed to pay 18 Lakh Rupees or one third of the tribute money to Salabat Jung. However, the Nizam refused to relent until the entire sum was paid. But then, there was news of a possible Maratha raid against Mysore. The Nizam fled Srirangapattana in a hurry. The news proved to be true. In March 1757, the Peshwa, Balaji Baji Rao attacked Mysore with a large force, easily subdued it, and demanded a hefty tribute. He received Five Lakh Rupees in cash and territory equivalent to the remaining twenty seven lakh Rupees.

The situation in Mysore had reached alarming proportions. The enmity between the Dalawai Nanjaraja and his brother Devaraja was costing the state dearly. Soldiers weren't paid their salaries on time, which led to a brewing revolt within the ranks. It was in these conditions that Hyder Ali was summoned to remedy the situation.

Hyder Ali left Dindigul and reached Mysore. The money he had looted in the past came to his aid now. He quickly put down the revolt-like situation in the army and imprisoned about 4000 men. He also seized the leaders of the revolt and plundered them. He paid the pending salaries of the soldiers. And then, step by step, he began to take over all the departments of the administration. He was now in a position of near-supreme authority.

From this position, he counseled against paying the remaining amount of the tribute owed to the Marathas. An infuriated Marathas sent a large contingent under the leadership of Gopal Hari who quickly captured Bangalore and marched towards Channapattana. When Hyder Ali heard this, he immediately deputed an army under his trusted lieutenant Lutf Ali Beg. The Marathas met with a surprise defeat at Channapattana after a pitched battle that lasted several months. Hyder Ali won this battle by thoroughly confounding the Maratha army with superior strategy and battle tactics. The Marathas finally agreed to release Bangalore and the pledged districts not without condition. Accordingly, Mysore had to pay a tribute of 32 Lakh Rupees to the Marathas. Half of this sum was immediately raised while Hyder Ali stood as the personal guarantor for the balance. The Maratha army returned. The role of the Marathi Brahmin, Khande Rao proved to be crucial in these negotiations. The Mysore Wodeyars expressed immense gratitude to Hyder Ali who had saved the kingdom from calamity and awarded him the title of *Fateh Hyder Bahadur*. Thus, Hyder who, until then was known as *Hyder Nayak* now became *Fateh Hyder*. However, Hyder Ali's eyes were set on a higher target.

The internecine conflict in the Mysore Kingdom, which had now reached a crescendo, only made things convenient for Hyder Ali. Chikka Krishnaraja Wodeyar was king only in name; the entire administration was in the hands of the minister, Nanjaraja. Fed up with this, the queen, who wanted to crush Nanjaraja, sent word for Hyder Ali through Khande Rao.

Hyder Ali readily accepted the offer and got rid of Nanjaraja quite easily. However, he replaced him. Chikka Krishnaraja Wodeyar was once again a puppet ruler. Almost all of the tax revenue of the Mysore State was in Hyder Ali's hands. More importantly, he had complete command over the army.

Once again, the Queen sent for Khande Rao who advised her to seek the support of the Marathas. The Marathas launched a direct attack on Srirangapattana. Taken by surprise, Hyder had to flee, leaving his family behind. With just a few followers, he managed to reach Bangalore, covering about 120 Kilometers in twenty hours. Hyder Ali had lost all his artillery and treasure and looked to his brother-in-law Makdum Ali for support. However, Makdum Ali was away, fighting a war in the Arcot district. It appeared as if Hyder Ali was completely doomed.

However, fortune smiled on him.

The Marathas were thoroughly routed by Ahmed Shah Abdali in the Third Battle of Panipat in 1761. As a result, its contingent at Mysore was hastily recalled to Poona. This was a huge relief for Hyder Ali who now proceeded towards Nanjangud where he encountered Khande Rao but was defeated and surrendered. Bowring's account of what transpired is worth recounting in full:

Haidar then adopted the singular course of throwing himself as a supplicant at the feet of Nanjaraj, the late Minister, who completely deceived by his professions of fidelity, was weak enough to put him in command of a respectable body of troops, and to give him the title of Dalawai. Armed with this authority, Haidar endeavoured to effect a junction with the force at [Srirangapattana] but was outmaneuvered by Khande Rao, and his ruin seemed inevitable. But he fabricated letters in the name of Nanjaraj to the officers of the latter's troops, desiring them to surrender Khande Rao in accordance with a pre-arranged agreement. These letters were designedly carried to Khande Rao, who fearing a conspiracy, abandoned his army, and fled to [Srirangapattana].

Haidar, hearing of Khande Rao's flight, attacked his troops, and gained an easy victory, capturing all his guns and baggage... For some months he was actively engaged [in preparations]...and when his preparations were complete, he assembled his army on the banks of the [River] Kaveri, opposite to [Srirangapattana]...After a few days...Haidar suddenly dashed across the river and surprised the enemy's camp...who at once acknowledged his authority. He then...demanded that the control of affairs [of the Mysore kingdom] be made over to him, and that...Khande Rao should be surrendered to his mercy.

Khande Rao met a truly painful end. Hyder promised that he would treat Khande Rao like a *tota* or parrot and honoured the promise. He imprisoned Khande Rao in an iron cage and fed him with only rice and milk till his death.

Hyder Ali Becomes the King of Mysore

The wheels of fortune had now fully turned in favour of Hyder Ali. Basalat Jung, the brother of the Nizam Salabat Jung was in charge of the affairs of the Adoni district. When Basalat Jung learnt of the defeat of the Marathas in North India, he planned an attack against Sira, which was under the Maratha control. Hyder Ali, who knew that it was beyond Basalat Jung's capability to singlehandedly attack

Hyder in talks with a British Official

Sira, assisted Basalat's expedition. Hyder Ali put a condition for rendering assistance: he had to be made the Nawab of Sira. However, Basalat Jung was merely the brother of the Nizam. He therefore didn't have the authority to make such a promise. Despite this, Basalat took three lakh rupees from Hyder Ali, and postwar, declared Hyder as the Nawab of Sira. Additionally, he conferred on him the title of *Hyder Ali Khan Bahadur*. After this, Hyder Ali began to openly address himself with this title.

Now, with renewed power and with Sira firmly under his control, Hyder Ali launched a series of raids against the tiny principalities. He crushed the Chikkaballapur, Rayadurga and Harapanahalli Palegars and extracted tributes from them. After this, he laid siege to the powerful principality of Chitradurga. While he was encamped there, he received a request for assistance.

Several centuries ago, the Nayakas had established a strong province at Keladi near Shimoga. Over time, they shifted their capital to Ikkeri. Much later, they shifted their base again to Bidanur after building a strong fort there. Shivappa Nayaka was the ruler of Bidanur (or Biduroor) in 1640. After the king Basavappa Nayaka died in 1755, his adopted son, a minor named Chennabasavayya was crowned as the king. This minor's guardian was the Queen Veerammaji. Very soon, a rumour arose that Veerammaji had conspired with her paramour and murdered the adopted son.

At this juncture, a prince who claimed to be Chennabasa-vayya came to Chitradurga and met Hyder Ali. He claimed that he was the heir to the Bidanur kingdom and requested Hyder Ali to help him secure the throne. Hyder Ali immediately left Chitradurga and proceeded to attack Bidanur, which was located in the dense jungles of Malnad. He occupied Shimoga and looted wealth amounting to some four lakh rupees. The Queen who was terrified of Hyder Ali's attack fled and hid in Ballalarayanadurga. However, Hyder Ali pursued her, attacked Ballalarayanadurga and finally imprisoned her in the jail at the Madhugiri fort. This expedition made Hyder richer by about twelve million pound sterling.

With Bidanur now under his control, Hyder contemplated making it his capital, and renamed it *Hyder Nagar*. He also planned to build a palace and a dockyard at the seacoast, which was close by. However, he received news of a rebellion brewing within his army. Wasting no time, he quelled it and imprisoned and executed about three hundred suspected rebels. Then he fell seriously ill. He realized that his hold over Mysore would weaken if he continued to stay at Bidanur.

Meanwhile, both the Marathas and the Nizam were seething with vengeance. The Marathas could not forget how Hyder had wrested Sira from them with the help of the Nizam's brother, Basalat Jung. On his part, the Nizam was furious that Hyder was strutting around, claiming that he was the Nawab, a sham title that Basalat Jung had conferred upon him.

Hyder correctly anticipated that an attack would emanate from either or both of these resenting parties. As a preemptive step, Hyder Ali tried to obtain the support of the Nawab of Savanur. When that failed, Hyder declared war on him and ravaged his country before finally seizing the fortress of Dharwad on the other side of the Tungabhadra River.

The Marathas wasted no time in sending their force to check Hyder Ali's rapid advances. Madhu Rao, the son of the Peshwa Baji Rao was the ruler of the Marathas in 1761. He sent a contingent headed by Gopal Rao, the chief of Miraj. Hyder Ali easily repelled Gopal Rao's army. An infuriated Madhu Rao sent the imperial Maratha Army, which roundly thrashed Hyder's force at Rattihalli. This was the second significant defeat in Hyder Ali's career. In fact, Hyder was so badly beaten that he had to flee into dense jungles of Bidanur with just a small cavalry to save his life. Meanwhile, monsoon broke out and impeded the progress of the Maratha army for a while. However, Madhu Rao was undaunted. He crossed the Tungabhadra River with his mammoth army and pursued Hyder vigorously. Hemmed in from all sides, a distraught Hyder Ali hurriedly transported his entire wealth and family members to Srirangapattana and sued for peace. As part of the terms of the peace agreement, he surrendered Gutti and Savanoor, which he had wrested from Murari Rao. He also agreed to pay thirty two lakh rupees as war reparations. However, Sira and other principalities, which he had raided and conquered, continued to remain in his control.

This defeat did not dishearten Hyder Ali. He now set

his eyes upon the Malabar region on the phony pretext that because it was near Bidanur, it belonged to him. He was helped in this endeavor by the invitation of a king named Ali Raja who ruled Cannanore. From there, he took out an expedition against the Samuri (Zamorin) of Calicut. However, he suffered a brief reversal at the hands of the Nair warriors who put up a fierce resistance. In the past, this selfsame Zamorin had requested the Mysore Wodeyar's help in a battle against the Raja of Palghat, and had taken Hyder Ali's army on loan. However, he had failed to pay the compensation due. Hyder Ali used this as the pretext to attack the Zamorin. Unable to withstand Hyder Ali's assault, the Zamorin surrendered and agreed to Hyder Ali's demands. Hyder Ali treated him with courtesy. The Zamorin however, took some time to arrange for funds, which made Hyder Ali suspicious. He thought the Zamorin was planning a conspiracy and imprisoned the Zamorin and his minister. Hyder Ali's brutal torture of the minister so frightened the Zamorin that he immolated himself.

Hyder then marched against the kings of Palghat and Kochi who surrendered without offering any resistance. After this, he marched towards Coimbatore. However, within three months of his departure, the Nair warriors rose in revolt. This forced Hyder Ali to return to the Malabar in a season of severe rains and overflowing rivers. The Nair force, which fell upon Hyder Ali's army inflicted major damage. It seemed as if Hyder Ali's army would suffer a horrific rout. However, thanks to the efforts and strategies of a French officer in Hyder Ali's army, the Nairs were decisively routed. Hyder Ali then resolved to teach an unforgettable lesson to all his enemies and potential rebels in the Malabar. He passed an order to behead or hang all war prisoners. Additionally, he rounded up thousands of Nairs and other innocent citizens and carted them off to Mysore. Thousands died en route due to fatigue and hunger.

This is just a small sample of Hyder Ali's cruelty.

Chikka Krishnaraja Wodeyar died in 1766. His elder son Nanjaraja was crowned as the successor according to Hyder Ali's orders. However, Hyder Ali was far away from Mysore. When he returned, he found that Nanjaraja had begun to make his own decisions and was asserting his authority as the Wodeyar. Hyder Ali immediately confiscated Nanjaraja's entire property, his personal estates and plundered his palace. He also took complete control of the Wodeyar's household affairs. In effect, he had declared himself as the king of Mysore. However, in his anger, he had forgotten the fact that such a forcible takeover of the state would invite the wrath of the Marathas.

Sure enough, the Marathas formed an alliance with the Nizam and marched towards Mysore. A panic-stricken Hyder sent Mehfooz Khan—elder brother of Muhammad Ali, the Nawab of Arcot—to sue for peace. The Peshwa refused to negotiate and marched onwards with his army.

Hyder Ali's cruelty was on display once again.

In a desperate bid to stop the progress of the Maratha army, he destroyed the embankments of reservoirs and poisoned wells and lakes. He brutally terrorized the peasantry and forcibly evacuated them from their villages. The plan was to deprive the Maratha army of food and water. However, the Maratha army under Madhu Rao was undaunted. It overcame all these hardships and at last laid siege to the fort at Sira, which was under the control of Mir Ali Raza Khan, Hyder's the brother-in-law. However, Raza Khan, instead of fighting with the Marathas surrendered to them. It looked as if Hyder's luck had finally run out.

However, at this crucial stage, Hyder Ali was saved by a man named Appaji Ram who was deputed by Hyder as an envoy. Appaji Ram approached Madhu Rao for negotiations and won the Peshwa's confidence through skillful diplomacy. In the end, Madhu Rao agreed to spare Hyder on the receipt of thirty two lakh rupees, and received half that sum immediately. For the remainder, Hyder Ali pledged Kolar. After some time, Madhu Rao received the balance and returned to Poona with his army. Hyder Ali was saved once again.

This then is the account of how Hyder Ali, a mere soldier and mercenary-for-hire, came to usurp the throne of the Mysore Wodeyars. Hyder Ali's meteoric rise to power can largely be attributed to two key factors: the chaotic political situation in South India and Hyder Ali's ruthless opportunism and mercenary character. His exploits were slightly better than the raids of a bandit. From beginning till end, Hyder did not consider himself loyal to anybody. Although he was identified with the Mysore army, he essentially did what he wanted. With a view on the throne of Mysore, he conducted unauthorized raids, defeated weak principalities and accumulated enormous loot. However, he was careful not to display his ambition till he was confident that his authority would be unchallenged.

In the end, he took advantage of the prevailing situation in the Wodeyar family and the Dalawai and usurped the throne of Mysore.

3

Betrayal of Madakari Nayaka and the Decimation of Chitradurga

After he became the unchallenged king of Mysore, Hyder Ali embarked on a series of wars with the British and the Marathas. His war with the British lasted from 1767-69. This time, he had managed to convince the Nizam Muhammad Ali to enter into an alliance with him. This two-year long battle was marked by reversals of fortunes for both parties at different points in time. When it appeared that the British had decisively gained the upper hand, the Nizam quickly dumped Hyder and allied with the British once again. In the end, however, Hyder Ali managed to prevail and extracted both territory and tribute from the British in an agreement dated 29 March 1769.

Meanwhile, the Marathas were preparing for a *fourth* invasion of Mysore. The fact that the important district of Sira was still in Hyder's possession, caused them resentment. Besides, Hyder had recently extracted hefty tributes from the Nawabs of Kadapa, Kurnool, and other smaller chiefs who owed allegiance to Sira.

As the Marathas advanced towards Mysore, Hyder Ali turned to the British for help. He was confident of their help given the treaty he had concluded recently. However, the British by now had realized that Hyder was not trustworthy and therefore ignored his request. Hyder knew that he was no match for the Marathas in an open battle and quickly retreated to his capital wasting the country as he went. Even before the war began, he sent an envoy to sue for peace. Madhu Rao demanded one crore rupees. Hyder rejected the terms upon which the Maratha army began to occupy his territory, invading all the northern and eastern districts, and establishing garrisons at major posts. However, Madhu Rao's unstoppable march was halted at the impregnable fort at Nijagal near Tumkur. Madhu Rao laid a fruitless siege to the fort for three months. In the end, he secured the help of Madakari Nayaka, the Palegar of Chitradurga. Madakari Nayaka's small band of brave Bedas scaled the fortress by escalade and managed to seize it. Madhu Rao then ordered the noses and ears of all the survivors of the fort to be cut off. However, he spared the life of the fort's commandant Sardar Khan because he was impressed by his courage and bravery.

A few days later, Madhu Rao became ill and had to return to Poona on the advice of his doctors. He instructed his maternal uncle Tryambak Rao to complete the unfinished business. The Maratha force continued its task of taking over Hyder Ali's territories and forced him to flee from place to place. He locked himself up in the strong fort of Savanadurga near Bangalore. However, the Maratha cannonaded the fort for eight days without respite forcing Hyder to flee once again. He was chased all the way up to Melukote, a short distance from Mysore. From here, he managed to somehow escape to the safety of Srirangapattana on 5 March 1771.

The Maratha army entered Srirangapattana effortlessly and laid siege to it for more than a year. Hyder finally sued for peace yet again and paid 15 lakh rupees and pledged some of his richest districts. During the course of the siege, Hyder learnt that Nanjaraj Wodeyar had been secretly communicating with the Marathas. As punishment, he ruthlessly ordered the Wodeyar to be strangled.

After the Marathas left, Hyder Ali set about restoring order to the affairs of Mysore. Eventually, he also managed to wrest some territories like Gutti, Bellary from the Marathas and then, invaded Coorg. However, he hadn't forgotten his revenge against Madakari Nayaka. Indeed, there were several reasons for Hyder's fury against this upstart Palegar of Chitradurga.

View of the Chitradurga Fort

Hyder's Wrath against Chitradurga

In the past, Chitradurga had been a feudatory of the Vijayanagar Empire. The Palegars (or chieftains) who ruled Chitradurga originally hailed from the Beda, or the hunter caste. During Bharamanna Nayaka's rule, it became a feudatory of the Mughal Empire. When the Mughals made Sira as one of their administrative center in South India, the Palegars of Chitradurga had to obey the whims of the imperial officers at Sira. Eventually, it passed into the hands of the Marathas. Then, Hyder Ali with the assistance of Basalat Jung wrested control of Sira. This spurred him on to launch the initial attack against Chitradurga. However, despite Hyder Ali's best efforts, he was simply unable to win Chitradurga. He laid siege for several months but the fort was simply impregnable.

Around this time, Hyder Ali received news that the combined forces of the Marathas and the Nizam were marching against him. Panic spread throughout Hyder Ali's army. With no alternative, Hyder made a hurried pact with Madakari Nayaka, extracted a token tribute and decamped from Chitradurga. One of the conditions of this pact was that Madakari Nayaka would send his troops to aid Hyder's battles against the Marathas and the Nizam.

Under the leadership of Hari Pant, the Maratha army comprising 60000 horsemen crossed the Tungabhadra River and camped at a place known as Raravi. Here, Hyder Ali managed to successfully create confusion in the Maratha army and managed to defeat it. It was also his *first* clear victory against the Marathas. He then captured the entire region between the Tungabhadra and Krishna rivers and returned to Mysore in 1779.

Madakari Nayaka had not sent his forces to help Hyder Ali. Apart from this, there was an even more important reason for Hyder's vendetta against Chitradurga. It was this same Palegar of Chitradurga who had sent his force of hunter-warriors to capture Hyder's fort at Nijagal. In other words, the puny Chitraduraga had dared to defy Hyder Ali on every occasion and despite his utmost exertions, had failed to capitulate. However, Hyder Ali had by then realized that he could not win Chitradurga in a direct confrontation. And so he decided to adopt a new tactic.

Chitradurga's army comprised some 3000 Muslim soldiers. Hyder Ali contacted them secretly by using the services of a Muslim fakir who acted as a mediator. The outcome was successful. The 3000 Muslim soldiers betrayed Madakari Nayaka from within the fort. Madakari Nayaka who became aware of this treachery at the last moment could really do nothing. Instead of surrendering, he fought valiantly and died in the battle. However, nothing would appease Hyder Ali's vengeance. In the words of Lewin Bowring,

*...Haidar, who, after plundering the place, despatched the [Palegar's] family to languish in prison at [Srirangapattana]. Haidar was determined to make short work of the brave Bedars who had so successfully fought against him, and heroically sacrificed their lives in defending their hereditary chief. Not content with confiscating all their available property, and ravaging the district for the support of his army, he carried off to his capital 20,000 of the inhabitants. The young boys were afterwards trained to arms, and formed the first nucleus of a band of compulsory converts from Hinduism to Islam; a band which was largely augmented in the reign of Tipu Sultan, under the title of the **Chela** or disciple battalions.* [Emphasis added]

This behavior on the part of Hyder Ali is reminiscent of his treatment of the Nair youth he had taken as prisoners during his Malabar raid. However, this was the first time that he had forcibly converted Hindus on such a massive scale. The Christian Missionary, Schwartz who visited Srirangapattana in 1779 has recorded this large-scale, forced conversion in his travelogue. Hyder Ali's officers tried to convince Schwartz that these "boys were destitute orphans whom Hyder had taken under his protection."

Hyder Ali who had been beaten by the Marathas *thrice,* beamed with pride because he had defeated Hari Pant. However, he couldn't reconcile himself with the humiliation of being unable to defeat a tiny principality like Chitradurga despite possessing a superior and numerically large military force. He had forgotten the fact that it was the people of the hunter caste—the same caste who ruled Chitradurga—who had played a key role in his victories. He had also forgotten that these hunter-warriors had helped him expand his army after he was promoted as the *Faujdaar* at Dindigul. He was bereft of any gratitude towards these loyal warriors who had stood by him in adversity. Even worse, he forcibly converted thousands of them to Islam.

4

Tipu Flogged by Hyder Ali

Tipu was born Fateh Ali Khan in 1753 at Devanahalli near Bangalore. His mother, Fakhr-un-Nissa was a daughter of the Governor of Kadapa, Mir Moinuddin. It is said that when the time of her delivery was fast approaching, she visited the shrine of a Muslim saint for whom Hyder Ali had a special veneration. The child was named after this saint.

The "Sultan" suffix was not conferred upon him for either becoming a king or for displaying feats of valour or courage. It was simply used as Tipu's last name.

As a young commander in his father's army, Tipu bossed over everyone including battle-hardened veterans. His words carried authority because he was Hyder Ali's son. However, both Hindus and Muslims who worked under this youngster quickly learned that he was a fanatical Muslim. From the beginning, Tipu imposed a strict schedule of daily prayers, abstinence from *haram* (forbidden) activities like drinking and gambling on every Muslim—no matter his rank—who reported to him. Those who were found guilty of violating his dictum were summarily dismissed from service. Tipu was also given to throwing highly temperamental fits and fickle mindedness, traits that his own father severely disapproved of.

The story of how this unstable young prince ascended the throne of Mysore and anointed himself as the *padshah*

A Portrait of Tipu Sultan

more or less begins with the episode of the public lashings he received from his father.

A Young Coward Deserts the Battlefield

This signal episode early in Tipu's life occurred when the Marathas invaded Mysore for the fourth time. It was during this expedition that they relentlessly chased Hyder Ali from place to place. He had lost almost all of his forts and was reduced to the status of a fugitive, constantly on the run just so he could save his life. When the Marathas battered even the secure fortress of Savanadurga, Hyder decided to flee to the safety of Srirangapattana via Melukote. Even to this day, Melukote is one of the most sacred places of pilgrimage for the Sri Vaishnava sect. To avoid detection, Hyder Ali's troops marched at night. However, on one occasion, Hyder had drunk excessively in the evening and was not in a position to lead his troops. It had been previously decided that Tipu was to lead the troops in the absence or inability of Hyder to do so. However, on this occasion, Tipu was nowhere to be found. Even worse, a soldier's gun accidentally went off and alerted the Maratha army. In Bowring's rather picturesque account,

...the Maratha cavalry aided by some guns which were brought to bear upon the enemy with great effect from the banks of a reservoir called the Pearl Tank, hovered in swarms about Haidar's infantry, which with much difficulty reached the hills near Chirkuli or Chinkurali. Here utmost confusion ensued, and during the panic the Maratha horse charged the fugitives...and commenced an indiscriminate slaughter. Seeing that all was lost...Haidar escaped alone...to [Srirangapattana], a distance of eleven miles.

Tipu separately reached Srirangapattana a few days later disguised as a Muslim fakir. The only soldier who behaved gallantly was an officer named Fazl Ullah Khan who gave a tough battle with his tiny unit, crossed the Kaveri River and reached Srirangapattana.

When Hyder Ali learned of how Tipu had intentionally fled from the battle scene and had later disguised himself as a fakir, he exploded in fury and ordered Tipu to be flogged publicly. This apart, Tipu was ordered to write an official letter of apology, nay, an *agreement*, an official undertaking, on which the seal was engraved in 1769. William Kirkpatrick's translation of the entire agreement is given below.

AGREEMENT

1. *I will not do [any] one thing without the pleasure of your blessed Majesty, Lord of Benefits [or my bountiful Lord]: if I do, let me be punished, in whatever manner may seem fitting to your auspicious mind.*

2. *If, in the affairs of the Sircar [Sarkar or Government], I should commit theft, or be guilty of fraud, great or small, let me, as the due punishment thereof, be strangled.*

3. *If I be guilty of prevarication, or misrepresentation, or of deceit, the due punishment thereof is this same strangulation.*

4. *Without the orders of the Presence [Hyder Ali], I will not receive from any one, Nuzzers [gifts or presents], &c.; neither will I take things from any one [forcibly]: if I do, let my nose be cut off, and let me be driven out from the city.*

5. *If, excepting on the affairs of the Sircar, I should hold conversation [probably cabal or intrigue] with any person, or be guilty of deceit, &c., let me, in punishment thereof, be stretched on a cross.*

6. *Whenever a country shall be committed to my charge by the Sircar, and an army be placed under my command, I will carry on all business regarding the same, with the advice, and through the medium of such confidential persons as*

> *may be appointed [for the purpose] by the Sircar; and if I
> transact such affairs through any other channel than this,
> let me be strangled.*

7. *If there should be any occasion for correspondence by
    writing, or to buy or give [away] anything, or any letters
    should arrive from any place, I will do nothing [in such
    matters] without the concurrence and advice of the person
    appointed by the Sircar.*

8. *I have written and delivered these few articles of my
    own free will: keeping the contents whereof in my heart's
    remembrance, I will act in each article accordingly. If I
    forget this, and act in any other [or different] manner, let
    me be punished, agreeably to the foregoing writing.*

Tipu was 21 years old when this incident occurred.
Neither is this the first instance of his cowardice. As we shall
see, Tipu either ran away from battle or meekly surrendered
whenever he was faced with challenging situations. And this
was apart from his habitual lying, breaking pacts, and going
back on his word.

Tipu's personality as assessed by his contemporaries

The punishment that Hyder Ali awarded and
subsequently, the apology letter that he demanded from Tipu
only show the esteem he held his son in. Indeed, Hyder was
fully aware of Tipu's character and mental makeup. As long
as he was alive, Tipu was not entrusted with any position
of importance in the administration or the military. By
virtue of being his son, Tipu was naturally given a suitably
high rank in the military but his job began and ended at
merely following Hyder's orders. Even there, Tipu proved
himself a failure. This fact calls the bluff of modern Tipu-
worshippers who glorify him as courageous, valiant, and
a master strategist. Contemporary British historians and

army officers who participated in the wars against Hyder Ali and Tipu have been consistent in their praise for Hyder as a "bold and enterprising commander, skillful in tactics... and never desponding in defeat." Equally, they have been consistent in portraying Tipu as "deficient in stability and straightforwardness, ferocious in character, cruel, bigoted..." and that "although he was a good rider and a skillful marksman, [he was] deficient in the capacity for war and [overconfident] in his own generalship [which] was often the cause of disaster and defeat."

Even when Hyder Ali was alive, the instances of Tipu leading army contingents and obtaining victory independently are far too few.

Indeed, Tipu's February 1782 victory against the British army led by Colonel Braithwaite was perhaps the only major milestone in his military career. However, the lion's share of the credit for this victory goes to the superior battle strategies devised by the French general M. Lally, who fought on Tipu's side. On September 6, Hyder Ali had dispatched an army commanded by Tipu against the British force led by Colonel Baillie. In this case, Tipu stumbled. Colonel Baillie's force marched onward towards Kanjeevaram from Perambakam. En route, Tipu attacked the British with an impressive show of artillery but his attack was easily repulsed. That night, Colonel Baillie decided to encamp instead of continuing his journey. This decision proved fateful. The next morning, Tipu had managed to recoup his scattered force and attacked Baillie's unit again. The British suffered considerable damage but quickly recovered thanks to the gallantry shown by Captains Rumley and Gowdie. Tipu's army was thoroughly routed yet again, and the British seized four cannons belonging to him. This reversal caused Hyder Ali to lead the charge from the front. In this battle too, M. Lally proved to be the master strategist. This time, Colonel Baillie was trounced. The fact that Hyder Ali—who 60 years old by then—had succeeded where his 20-something son had not speaks volumes, and needs no further explanation.

Hyder Ali dies

About a month or two after this, Hyder Ali decided to reestablish his supremacy in the Malabar and Coorg. As part of this expedition, he sent a large contingent under the leadership of Tipu. The British too sent their contingent from Bombay too meet Tipu who was stationed near Panniani (or Ponani) near Calicut. Hyder himself had encamped at a distance of about 16 miles north of Arcot. His health however, had badly declined by then. He was suffering from a carbuncle on his back which in the words of La Toure and John Hasz (quoted in *Tipu Sultan* by Denneys Forest) was "as large as a dinner plate."

Despite the best efforts of his physicians, Hyder Ali succumbed to the ailment on 7 December 1782 at Narasingarayanapet.

5

Tipu's Ascent to Power

Perhaps Hyder Ali didn't anticipate his death so soon. It could also be that his dominating presence prevented any possibility of succession battles or palace intrigue. However, it is a fact of history that he had not openly declared Tipu as his successor. In any case, he had a low opinion of Tipu's abilities and competence.

However, because he died suddenly and a war was underway, the mantle of leading the entire Mysore army naturally fell on Tipu's shoulders. That still did not automatically mean that he would become the sovereign of Mysore. The story of how he took over the throne of Mysore owes to two trusted ministers of Hyder Ali, Diwan Purnayya and Krishna Rao with a little help from the French in Hyder's pay. These men had correctly assessed the fact that Hyder would not survive his illness but kept their assessment secret. Immediately after his death, they dispatched messengers to Tipu who had encamped at Panniani in Kerala. Meanwhile, they had also embalmed Hyder Ali's body and had arranged for it to be transported in utmost secrecy to Kolar in a coffin, which resembled a treasure chest. His palanquin was sealed shut and was carried about as usual. Those who questioned this were told that Hyder's ailment would intensify if he was exposed to sunlight.

Meanwhile, Tipu traversed the distance of 280 miles from Panniani to Chittoor in just four days. He was greeted by the soldiers with great joy, and he assumed control of the affairs immediately. News of Hyder Ali's death was finally revealed when his body reached the capital, Srirangapattana. The other, carefully hidden strategy was to ensure that there would be no impediment to Tipu's ascension. Indeed, the letter written and jointly signed by Purnayya, Krishna Rao and other highly-trusted confidants addressed Tipu as follows:

To the Exalted Presence of that offspring of posperity and honour; the Tree bearing fruit of dignity and majesty, the Conqueror of the world, Tipu Sultan Bahadur.

This letter was delivered to Tipu at Panniani by Maha Mirza.

Purnayya's strategy was such a grand success that even the British didn't suspect that anything was amiss.

Character differences between father and son

There was a marked contrast in the personalities of Hyder Ali and Tipu.

Hyder Ali was an incurable debauch. Although Tipu fathered 11 children, he wasn't all that interested in women. Hyder Ali was a constant fixture at parties that involved liquor and debauchery. Tipu however, was engaged in reading the Quran and/or performing religious activities in his leisure hours. Tipu had a fanatical zeal for Islam, and called his kingdom *Khudaadaad Sarkar (The Kingdom Bestowed by God)*. Similarly, he called his army the "Holy Camp." He showered such epithets upon himself as the "Tiger of the Kingdom Bestowed by God," and called his administration as the *Hyderi (Lion-like) Administration*. Hyder Ali on the other hand, was extremely ambitious and pursued his goal of extending his kingdom as far as possible. He exhibited his savagery on occasion but displayed none of the fanatical Islamic bigotry that Tipu did throughout his reign. The British Colonel, historian, and scholar, William Kirkpatrick who discovered more than 2000 letters (written in Farsi in Tipu's own handwriting) at the Srirangapattana fort after Tipu's death makes a devastating assessment of Tipu's character and personality:

The importance of these letters...consist[s]...in the vivid illustration which they afford of the genius, talents, and disposition of their extraordinary author, who is here successively and repeatedly delineated, in colors from his own pencil, as the cruel and relentless enemy; the intolerant bigot or furious fanatic; the oppressive and unjust ruler; the harsh and rigid master ; the sanguinary tyrant; the perfidious negotiator; tile frivolous and capricious innovator; the mean and minute economist; the peddling trader; and even the retail shop-keeper...the various murders and acts of treachery, which we see him directing to be carried into execution, were not criminal, but...just, and even meritorious, in his eyes. They might... in a great degree, proceed from a disposition naturally cruel and sanguinary: but, perhaps, an intolerant religious zeal and bigotry were not less active motives to them...the Sultan does not appear to have possessed a sufficient stretch of thought upon any subject...to enable him to discuss it, either with logical force or precision. A consecutive train of argument was a thing of which he nowhere seems to have had an idea... Arrogance and vanity were, undoubtedly, among the most prominent features of the Sultan's mind.

As we shall see, Kirkpatrick was more than accurate in his assessment of Tipu.

6

The Durbar of an Islamic Fanatic

As soon as he assumed power, Tipu unleashed a series of bigoted policies throughout his kingdom. There is a veritable treasure of evidence both in terms of the number and extent of the kind of fanatical durbar Tipu ran during his 17-year long regime.

In 1786, Tipu declared himself the *Padshah*. After this momentous occasion, he took an extreme liking for flattery and surrounded himself with sycophants and time-servers. Tipu also regarded himself as the protector of Islam and went to extreme lengths to make the world aware of this fact.

During that period, several Nawabs, Nizams, and other Muslim feudatories still owed allegiance to the horribly-dwindled power of the Mughals. All mosques throughout India read the daily prayer or *Qutba* in the name of the current Mughal Emperor. However, Tipu issued an order that mandated all the mosques in his dominions to read the *Qutba* in his name. Tipu's objective behind issuing this order was two fold: one, to run the administration of his kingdom strictly according to the tenets of Islam, and two, to send a message to the world that he was the protector of Islam.

Renames Places, Wrecks the Economy, and Weakens the Military

The other manifestation of the same objective was his exercise of renaming all the places under his control. He renamed the coastal region under his control as *Yaamsubaa*,

Tipu Sultan - Another Portrait

the densely-forested Malnad as *Taransubaa,* and the plains of Karnataka as *Ghabraasubaa.* He also changed the names of cities and towns and introduced these new names in all administrative records and documents.

The following is a partial list of the places he renamed.

Existing Name	Renamed by Tipu to
Mysore	Nazarbad
Mysore Ashtagrama	Isaar (Southern region)
Srirangapattana Ashtagrama	Aimun (Northern region)
Mangalore	Jalalabad
Dharwad	Khurshid-Sawad
Hassan	Khayimabad
Honnavar	Saddaihasgad
Kundapur	Nasrullabad
Ballapura	Azmathshukoh
Gurramakonda	Jaffarabad
Gutti (Gooti)	Faiz-Hissar
Molakalmuru	Mohammadabad
Kozhikode (Calicut)	Islamabad
Dindigul	Kalikabad
Madikeri	Jaffarabad
Bidanur	Nagar or Haidar Nagar
Sadashivgad	Majidabad
Satyamangalam	Salamabad
Pavangad	Hafizabad
Devanahalli	Yusufabad
Krishnagiri	Fulk-ul-Azam
Ratnagiri	Mustafabad
Chakragiri	Asifabad

Chandragiri	Shukoorabad
Nandidurga	Gurdoom Shukoh
Chitradurga	Farooq yab hissar
Maharayadurga	Asabarabad
Kavaledurga	Iskeezh ghar
Kabbaladurga	Jaaffoorabad
Devarayanadurga	Ballashukoh
Beeranadurga	Azimabad
Mekeridurga	Fullokh Shukoh
Holeyurudurga	Ifarabad
Sira	Rustumabad
Basrur	Vazirabad
Dhanayakakote	Husseinbad
Aandiyuru	Ahmadabad
Bekal	Rumutabad
Sakaleshpur	Manjrabad
Chandragutti	Shukurabad

In his zeal to give Islamic names to existing cities and towns, Tipu gave the *same* name to different places causing great confusion.

After his defeat and death in 1799, the British, who took over the Mysore administration, had a tough time trying to straighten the revenue records. William McLeod who was the Superintendent of the Land Revenue department shows us several facets of Tipu's bigoted durbar. He has documented in meticulous detail the kind of mess Tipu had created, thanks to his fanatical love of Islam.

McLeod discovered that the list of the chiefs of every province or district contained only Muslim names like Sheikh Ali, Sher Khan, Muhammad Syed, Meer Hussain, Syed Peer,

Abdul Karim, and so on. There was nary a Hindu or non-Muslim name. Twenty districts of Tipu's dominions were subdivided into 1075 Amaldaaris (Administrative units), each overseen by an Amaldaar. All of these were headed by Muslims. McLeod made an exhaustive study of the revenue and taxation system implemented by Tipu and found that tax revenue during Tipu's rule had sunken to deplorable levels. The following is a partial list of the revenues accruing from the major districts in Tipu's kingdom:

District	Tax Revenue (Pagodas)
Mysore (Nazarbad)	214600
Gooty (or Gutti or Faiz Hissar)	284150
Bidanur	341630
Ashtragram (near Mysore)	326110

Revenue from other districts was negligible. One major reason for the steep decline in revenue in the words of William McLeod was the fact that

All the Amildars under Tipu's Government were Moors who were seldom chosen for any other reason than their being Muhammadans; and although they had an oath of fidelity administered to them, the embezzlement of public revenue, by the several classes of servants, is supposed to have amounted annually to 15 or 20 lakhs of pagodas.

The British discontinued the coin and currency system introduced by Tipu and revived the earlier Pagoda and Rupee system.

M.H. Gopal's excellent *Tipu Sultan's Mysore: An Economic Study* published in 1971 echoes McLeod:

Even in the Revenue Code...Tipu exhibited his communal tendencies. Mussulmans were exempted from paying the house

tax, and taxes on grain and other goods meant for their personal use and not for trade. Christians were seized and deported to the capital, and their property confiscated. Converts to Islam were given concessions such as exemption from taxes... If a person who converted to Islam was a peasant, he was entitled to a 50% tax rebate on his agricultural income. He was completely exempt from house tax. Lands seized from various persons as well as Government lands were given to Qazis and other Muslim officers as "Inaam" (gift). Lands were freely gifted away for the purpose of constructing Mosques. On the other hand, lands given to temples and Brahmins were taken back.

Indeed, it was Tipu's morbid obsession with Islamizing his entire kingdom that wrecked the economy. This is of course, apart from his incessant and thoughtless raids and costly defeats at the hands of the British and their allies. A significant expression of this morbid obsession was the appointment of only Muslims to high posts in various departments of his administration. Of the 65 *Asfs* (Revenue Officers) and assistant *Asfs* in his employ, not one was a Hindu. Most of these officers were illiterate apart from being incompetent. Sometimes, these revenue officers were promoted to high positions such as a *Mir* (commander) in the military. In the words of M.H. Gopal,

Another evil which later assumed huge proportions was the appointment of inexperienced people as officers and the lenience with which he sometimes treated them. In 1785 he ordered his Diwan of Bangalore not to take rigid measures to recover the balance due from Mir Futah Ali, the talukdar of Chikkaballapur, but to realise it gradually as the officer "has never before exercised the functions of that office, and...he is...a stranger and inexperienced in business." As Kirkpatrick remarks, this "necessarily brings in question the prudence of the Sultan, whom we see placing men in trust, to which he knew them to be unequal."

This sordid state of affairs was compounded by Tipu's love for the Farsi language. Before Tipu assumed power, Kannada was the medium of (writing) accounts in the revenue department. Typically, revenue officers would write accounts in Kannada and send fair copies to the *Amildars* who had them translated to Marathi. Copies in both languages would be kept. However, Tipu abolished this practice and made Farsi the medium of accounts throughout his kingdom. This move ostensibly was to help his handpicked Muslim officers who only knew Farsi. And it was true. They knew just that—the Farsi language—and were complete failures in the matters of revenue administration.

Thus, thanks to Tipu's rabidly communal policy of appointing people to high positions regardless of merit, he successfully managed to—in the words of M.H. Gopal— subvert the "wise and economical system established by his father." Gopal further quotes a contemporary of Tipu as saying that it is

An ascertained fact that he (Tipu) has not collected so much from his country as his father, a circumstance which may be [ascribed] to his chiefly employing Mussulman assofs and amildars which Hyder seldom did.

Neither did his communal policy of employment stop at administration. It extended even to the military with predictably disastrous consequences. We have a sample of this in the story of a Brahmin from Kolar who was forcibly converted to Islam and given the name of Khan Jahan, and promoted to a high office in the military. Inexperienced in warfare and lacking the competence required for the position of a *Mir Miran* (commander), Khan Jahan's performance had deadly consequences for Tipu's troops at Coorg as we shall see. However, Khan Jahan was not the exception but the rule of appointing and promoting people purely on religious grounds even in the military. In a short time, important positions in Tipu's army were occupied by people who had no competence or experience and lacked the kind of courage required for a soldier.

The following revealing account comes from Mir Hussein Kirmani, the official hagiographer-cum-biographer-cum-sycophant of Tipu. Kirmani's biography of Tipu titled *Nishan-i-Haidari* was translated from Farsi to English by Colonel Mark Wilkes.

The kind and friendly Sultan sat at one table with all the Amirs and soliders...ate his dinner and said that...they were all brethren in religion...and it was indispensable that all jealousy and enmity should be cast aside from their minds.

Tipu's bigoted scheme of appointment also had a darker side. This was the formation of the *Ahmadi* (God's) contingent. This contingent consisted of the unfortunate Hindu youths who were imprisoned during Tipu's savage campaigns at Mangalore, the Malabar, and Coorg. These youths were transported to Srirangapattana, circumcised, converted to Islam, and conscripted. Tipu then created a dedicated contingent which consisted of only such unfortunate souls. He named this the *Ahmadi* contingent.

Butchers the Metric System, the Calendar, and Currency

Lewin B Bowring in his *Haidar Ali and Tipu Sultan* gives a detailed account of the insane extent of Tipu's obsession with Islam. It is worth quoting the original.

Measures of distance too were amended, the kos or Indian two-miles being now defined as consisting of so many yards of twice twenty-four thumb-breadths, because the creed (Kalmah) contains twenty-four letters. The kos thus fixed was 2¾ miles, and if the letter-carriers did not travel this distance in 33 minutes they were to be flogged. All the names of weights and measures were altered.

But the most wonderful of his improvements was his new method of calculating time. As is well known, the Hindus counted time in cycles of 60 years, each year having a separate name, a system which makes their chronology somewhat difficult to unravel. Tipu founded a new calendar on this basis, giving however fantastic names to the years, and equally strange ones to the lunar months. The year, according to his arrangement, only contained 354 days, and each month was called by some name in alphabetical order. From the year 1784, all his letters were dated according to the day of one or other of the months in this new nomenclature.

Tipu introduced his new calendar in the fifth year of his rule. However, this calendar wasn't the traditional Islamic calendar. Unlike the Islamic *Hijri* calendar, Tipu's calendar begins with the year of the birth of the Prophet Muhammad. Most historians and contemporaries of Tipu aver that this bizarre idea must have been planted inside Tipu's head by the bigoted Islamic scholars and other Muslim religious leaders who filled Tipu's court. Apart from assigning Arabic names for years, months, and days, Tipu introduced a new system of reading the year number from the right to the left. The names assigned to years by Tipu were equally outlandish: *Ahand, Ab, Jha, Baab,* and so on.

Tipu also issued a new system of coinage, fashioned again by his fixation with Islam. He engraved the following words on the obverse of these coins: *"the faith of Ahmad (Muhammad) is proclaimed to the world by the victories of Haidar struck in Pattan [Srirangapattana] in the year Jalu or 1199 Hijri."* On the reverse were engraved, *"He* [it is unclear whether it refers to God or Tipu] *is the only Sultan, the just one the third of Bahari in the year Jalu, and third of the reign."*

Although the Mughal Empire had by then declined irreversibly, the coins minted by the Mughals were still widely in currency. Tipu showed the audacity to send the coins, which he had minted, as gifts to the Mughal Emperor. To compound the arrogance, these coins had omitted the name of the Mughal Emperor. The Mughal Emperor, Shah Alam was livid. Tipu quickly realized his blunder, and in the words of Bowring, "pretended that he had merely sent the coins in order to ascertain His Majesty's pleasure about them, and offered an apology for the affront."

He gave the names of Muslim saints to coins minted in gold and silver. To copper coins, he gave Arabic and Farsi names, and named them after stars. *Pagoda* was the name of a coin that was in common circulation during that period. Tipu renamed *Pagoda* to *Ahamadi* because it was one of the names of the Prophet. Further, he gave the name *Sadiq* to a coin whose value was two Pagodas. Tipu's reasoning? *Sadiq* was the name of the First Caliph. According to this new numismatic nomenclature, the one-paisa coin was called *Zehra*, the two-paise, *Outmaani*, and so on. In several instances, he gave new names for coins that he himself had renamed earlier: *Farooqi, Jaffar,* and *Imami,* for instance. There was also a Rupee named *Hyder.*

Neither did he spare the world of weights and measures. He altered long-established names and systems such as *Abjud, Hauz,* and *Hutti.* These were now given Islamic names such as *Ahamadi, Bihari, Julwa, Darai,* and *Hashimi.*

An Obsessive Writer and an Incompetent Administrator

Tipu was an obsessive-compulsive writer, and wrote prolifically on every conceivable subject.

Although he was the king, Tipu was not the one to delegate even a task as mundane as writing a simple letter. On the contrary, his letters were neither simple nor brief. He often wrote highly detailed letters to both his civil and military officers. These letters were loaded with elaborate instructions, advice, and recommendations. No area escaped his attention, and no affair was minor. He wrote on military operations, general regulations, and even petty trading. Even in specialized subjects like medicine, commerce, economics, religious observances, engineering, and military science, Tipu held forth his opinions as if they were settled truths. This despite the fact that he had little or no knowledge or background required to understand these difficult subjects.

Tipu had an immense love for the Farsi language. He was schooled in the language and could read and write in Farsi. His written Farsi was tolerable, and he signed his letters with the *Nabbi Malik* (the Prophet is the Master) suffix.

Because Tipu labored under the illusion that he was the Master on military matters, he wrote "*The Triumphs of Holy Warriors,*" a book comprising 18 chapters. The book contained detailed instructions and guidance on things like exercises for soldiers, the duties of all grades of officers, night attacks, fighting in a forest region or on plains, salutes on special occasions, military guards, furlough, desertions, and so on. According to an ordinance (*Hukmnamah*) issued by Tipu in 1793, the *Piadah Askar*, or regular infantry, comprised five *Kachahris* or divisions, and twenty-seven *Kashuns* or regiments. Each *Kashun* contained 1,392 men (of whom 1,056 carried muskets) with an adequate staff, both combatant and non-combatant. A *Jauk*, or company of rocket men, was attached to each *Kashun*, and also two guns.

The cavalry force was divided into three units: (1) Regular Cavalry where the Government provided the horses, (2) *Silahdars* who provided their own horses, and (3) *Kazzaks*, or Predatory Cavalry. The first category or the Regular Cavalry called *Sawar Askar*, comprised three *Kachahris* or divisions, comprising each, six *Mokabs* or regiments of 376 troopers. This apart, the *Silahdars* mustered 6,000 horses, and the *Kazzaks* 8,000.

However, Tipu failed to implement these outlandish edicts. In the end, they fell in the realm of the ridiculous.

In 1796, Tipu embarked on an ambitious project of building a massive naval force. To this end, he constituted a Board of Admiralty comprising 11 persons and bestowed the *Mir Yam (Sea Lord)* title upon them. Each *Mir Yam* had about 30 warriors known as *Mir Bahar (Commander)* under him. The navy was planned to consist of twenty line-of-battle ships, and twenty large frigates. Six of each class of ships were to be stationed at Mangalore, seven at Wajidabad near the Mirjan creek, and seven at Majidabad or Sadashivgarh. Tipu also wrote details about the number and type of guns to be installed on each ship, and the class of soldiers (this also included the details of their salary) that would be stationed on them.

However, even in this case, the plan remained on paper.

Tipu also displayed his Islamic orthodoxy in administrative and civil matters. Without considering the feelings, traditions, and customs of the locals and the impact on the economy, he ordered the prohibition of alcohol in his dominions. The prohibition extended even to the manufacture of liquor. However, he made an exception for his loyal French ally, General M. Lally, who opened a shop in his camp for selling liquor. The sale could only be made to the French soldiers who were in Tipu's service. In 1787, Tipu wrote a letter to the local official at Bangalore ordering him to take written agreements from both the vendors and distillers of alcohol to give up their profession and engage in other occupations. Similar orders were issued throughout his territory.

These are but a few instances that reveal how Tipu operated mostly in the realm of fantasy. It goes without saying that every attempt at enforcing his fantasies in the real world ended up as disasters and caused immense misery for his subjects. This was not merely because Tipu was an incompetent administrator, a fact which his father, Hyder Ali had noticed very early.

The petty-minded Sultan

Tipu lacked even the most basic and common attributes of a king—large heartedness and dignity of conduct. These attributes were instead replaced by pettiness and temperamental behavior. Hyder Ali had never compromised on the welfare of his soldiers—he gave them generous salaries and made ample provisions for their food and clothing. Tipu on the other hand would constantly rant about the expense incurred for clothing and feeding his troops, and even at the number of wax-candles needed for ship-stores. He once castigated an officer who complained of being supplied with old and black rice.

Tipu failed as an administrator because of his obsession with Islam and his penchant for grandiose daydreaming. Constantly preoccupied with the matters of religion, he neglected administration. He spent the early years of his rule devising and implementing policies which would help him fashion all aspects of the State according to the diktats of Islam. His Islam-obsession was supplemented by his constant quest for bizarre innovations.

Thus, Tipu's policies were notable for their eccentricity and calamitous in their implementation. However, all this appears comparatively harmless, childish even, when we examine his political and expansionist record, which reveals a truly macabre side of the Sultan.

7

The Savage Sultan

Lewin Bowring mentions a "remarkable proclamation" that Tipu issued in 1786,

> ...calling upon all true believers to 'extract the cotton of negligence from the ears of their understanding,' and, quitting the territories of apostates and unbelievers, to take refuge in his dominions, where, by the Divine blessing, they would be better provided for than before, and their lives, honour, and property remain under the protection of God," and that he had resolved that the "worthless and stiff-necked infidels, who had turned aside their heads from obedience to the true faith, and openly raised the standard of unbelief, should be chastised by the hands of the faithful, and made either to acknowledge the true religion or to pay tribute. As, owing to the imbecility of the princes of Hind, that insolent race (presumably the English) had conceived the futile opinion that true believers had become weak, mean, and contemptible, and had overrun and laid waste the territories of Musalmans, extending the hand of violence and injustice on the property and honour of the faithful, he had resolved to prosecute a holy war against them.

This vitriolic broadside was initially disseminated in the dominions under his control. After some time, he issued another order to propagate this vitriol in various places in the Nizam's territory with the objective of provoking all True Believers to join his Jihad whose goal was to expel the British from India. Tipu reserved a special hatred for the Nizam whom he regarded as an apostate and called him a barber and "the son of a worthless mother" for siding with the Marathas and the British.

In this connection, he wrote a letter to the Mughal Emperor, which read as follows:

This steadfast believer, with a view to the support of the firm religion of Muhammad, undertook the chastisement of the Nazarene tribe, who, unable to maintain the war I waged against them, solicited peace in the most abject manner. With the divine aid and blessing of God, it is now again my steady determination to set about the total extirpation and destruction of the enemies of the faith.

It is clear that Tipu made no secret of hiding his real intent.

And when he put his intent into practice, it became brutally clear what he was really capable of. Indeed, Tipu's religious zealotry is matched only by his extraordinary cruelty. The present day devotees of Tipu only need to look at a fraction of the volumes of firsthand accounts left behind by the British, and the Rajas and Nawabs who bore the brunt of Tipu's "fight for India's freedom." Even worse, Tipu, the obsessive-compulsive letter-writer, basked in immense self-pride and celebrated his barbarism as marvelous triumphs in the service of Islam in the letters he wrote to his military officers. Indeed, almost every account on Tipu written by the British who participated in action against him is consistent in describing the abominable mercilessness that he displayed. The narratives of Tipu's cruelty are gut-wrenching. Neither do we have any paucity of material on this barbarian. Despite all this, one wonders how and why Tipu is today painted almost as a saint.

His wanton campaigns against various Rajas, Nawabs, and Chieftains throughout his reign provide ample proof of the extreme barbarity he could unleash. His raids in

Mangalore, the Malabar, and Coorg are vicious samples of this fact. The atrocities that he and his soldiers committed on the innocent citizens of a place he captured were truly horrifying. Apart from looting the conquered territory comprehensively, Tipu used to horribly torture and kill innocent people *en masse*; those who managed to survive were forcibly converted to Islam. Indeed, he had formed a separate unit of horsemen named *Khazakh* dedicated to this very purpose. The officers, soldiers, and other prisoners who fell into his hands were destined for a truly miserable fate. His prison at Srirangapattana was filled with thousands of people he had captured in his raids at Mangalore, the Malabar, and Coorg. The Englishmen he had captured were brutally, ceaselessly tortured for days before they were killed. In Bowring's words,

Tipu...had no compunction in cutting [the prisoners'] throats, or strangling and poisoning them; while...numbers of them were sent to die of malaria and starvation on the fatal mountain of Kabaldrug [Kabbaladurga]. The English prisoners were specially selected as victims of his vengeance, not omitting officers of rank such as General Matthews; while, in direct contravention of the treaty made at Mangalore in 1784, he did not scruple to retain in captivity considerable numbers of Europeans. Many of these, particularly young and good-looking boys, were forcibly circumcised, married haphazard to girls who had been captured in the Coromandel districts, and drafted into the ranks of the army, or compelled to sing and dance for the amusement of the sovereign... those who conspired against him were put in a cage... [and] were allowed half a pound of rice a day, with salt, but no water, so they soon expired under this frightful ordeal.. There were other punishments nearly equally dreadful, such as making men bestride a wooden horse on a saddle studded with sharp spikes. On a spring being touched the horse of torture reared, and the spikes penetrated the unfortunate wretches. A more common mode of punishment was to bind tightly

the hands and feet of condemned men, and then to attach them by a
rope to the foot of an elephant, which, being urged forwards, dragged
them after it on the rough ground, and painfully terminated their
existence. Some again were ruthlessly thrown into the dens of tigers
to be devoured.

Nandidurga (now known as Nandi Hills) near Bangalore has an imposing cliff on the summit in the south-west direction. This is now known as "Tipu's Drop," owing to a tradition where prisoners were hurled over it by orders of Tipu. Indeed the appellation, "Tipu's Drop" is simply a mirror to Tipu's cruelty.

Hayavadana Rao, author of the *Mysore Gazetteer* mentions an account of how Tipu defeated the Palegar of Bellary through treachery, looted the city, and utterly destroyed the fort. In the same account, he also records a very revealing incident. Calicut was one of the important cities that fell prey to Tipu's savagery during his raid in the Malabar. Tipu's sack of Calicut was accompanied by an order of razing the entire city to the ground. On this occasion, Tipu's fanaticism had reached such truly insane levels that he declared himself to be the Prophet Muhammad!

Tipu's numerous handwritten letters are themselves firsthand proofs of his cruelty. In letters written to his commander Burhan-ud-din during the 1786 Maratha war, Tipu reveals the true face of his inhuman nature. In one such letter, he directs Burhan to cross the Tungabhadra from Anavatti, as follows:

You must leave the women and other rubbish, together with
the superfluous baggage of your army, behind.

During the same war, he wrote a letter to the head of a regiment, which had laid siege to Naragund:

In the event of your being obliged to assault the place, every
living creature in it, whether man or woman, old or young, child,

dog, cat, or anything else, must be put to the sword, with the single exception of Kala Pandit (the commandant).

In another letter, addressed to an officer in Coorg, Tipu remarks:

You are to make a general attack on the Coorgs, and, having put to the sword or made prisoners the whole of them, both the slain and the prisoners, with the women and children, are to be made Musalmans.

Again, in an uprising against Tipu at Supa in the Canara region, Tipu instructs his general, Badruz Zaman Khan as follows:

Ten years ago, from ten to fifteen thousand men were hung upon the trees of that district; since which time the aforesaid trees have been waiting for more men. You must therefore hang upon trees all such of the inhabitants of that district as have taken a lead in these rebellious proceedings.

The tenor of this letter in itself is extremely savage. Compared to this, the letter that Tipu wrote to Arshad Beg Khan who was in charge of quelling a revolt in Calicut is slightly milder.

Such of the authors of this rebellion and flagrant conduct as have been already killed, are killed. But why should the remainder of them, on being made prisoners, be put to death? Their proper punishment is this: Let the dogs, both black (Hindus) and white (the British), be regularly despatched to Seringapatam.

In yet another letter, written on the occasion of seizing a part of the Nizam's calvary at Kadapa, Tipu says:

Let the prisoners be strangled, and the horses, after being valued, be taken into Government service.

Colonel William Kirkpatrick's collection of Tipu's letters contains numerous such letters where Tipu in his own hand, exulted in the savage deeds he committed and ordered others under him to commit.

The Suspicious Sultan

The Persian scholar Colonel William Miles who translated Mir Hussain Kirmani's hagiography on Tipu writes in the preface of his translation that

[Tipu] was a bigoted Muslim, and like most of that class unprincipled and quite unscrupulous as to the means he employed to attain his ends in the propagation of his religion. With these bad qualities, his dark, suspicious, faithless character, alienated those who were at first his most attached friends, and at the time Srirangapattana was taken [in the Fourth Anglo-Mysore War], *he appears to have had scarcely one [friend] left.*

A close reading of Tipu's career reveals how accurate Miles' was in his assessment of Tipu. Apart from intense religious bigotry, Tipu was endowed with a highly suspicious nature bordering on paranoia. He never trusted anybody and used to oppress even those who were loyal to him. He employed spies to track every movement of the top officials in his administration and military. Here is Bowring's description of the Police State Tipu had created:

...the Sultan...owing to the deep distrust which he entertained even against his principal officials, whose families were compelled to reside permanently at the capital...In order to ascertain what went on in their households, the police were directed ' to place spies in the fort, in the town of Ganjam adjoining it, in the bazars, and over the doors of the great Mirs, so as to gain intelligence of every person who went to another's house and of what was said, thereby acquiring an accurate knowledge of the true state of things, to be reported daily to the Presence.' It was at the same time forbidden that any one should go to the house of another to converse. [Emphasis added]

In other words, the compulsion of the officials' families to reside in Srirangapattana was a little less than an open threat to those who contemplated falling out of line. And it's not just that. We have proof, in Tipu's own hand as to what would occur in case officials met each other in the absence, or without the knowledge of this suspicious Sultan. Letter Number 276 in Colonel William Kirkpatrick's collection reads as follows:

You must not suffer any one to come to your house; and whatever business you may have to do, let it be transacted in our Kuchurri [office]. Nevertheless, people should persist in coming to your house; they shall be deprived of their ears and noses. Pay strict attention to this order.

This was written to Muhammad Mehdy, a *bakshi* (a title given to someone senior in the administration or military) in Tipu's court. Kirkpatrick's observations on the letter are equally interesting

This order...would amount to the exclusion of every person from the habitation of the bakshi, who might occasionally have private business with him: but though the regulation, directing all public affairs to be transacted in open Kuchurry, and nowhere else, was rigidly enforced by the Sultan, it can hardly be supposed, that it was meant to extend to the mutual intercourse necessary in the conduct of personal or domestic concerns."

Neither was this paranoia new. It dated back to his formative years. The fate of Ayaz Khan, the governor of Bidanur is a classic, if cruel, illustration of Tipu's psychosis. Ayaz Khan was originally a Nair from Malabar who was captured and forcibly converted by Hyder Ali. Over time, Hyder developed a lasting affection for him and regarded him like a son. After the Bidanur expedition where he obliterated the Nayaka dynasty, Hyder appointed Ayaz Khan as the Governor of the principality. On another occasion, Hyder severely reprimanded Tipu, calling him a liar and a cheat and a coward, and said that he would've been happier if Ayaz Khan had been his biological son. Tipu never forgot this. And so, after he assumed power, he declared that Ayaz Khan was a traitor and quoting a Persian verse, said that "excessive rain is as bad as lightning to the crops or harvest." This was in reference to Ayaz being the governor of a hugely wealthy and prosperous province like Bidanur. Further, Tipu said that Ayaz was a "slave and wicked man, determined to destroy the foundations of the prosperity of his patron and master." Ayaz Khan got the message. He realized that his position was no longer safe under Tipu's dispensation and decamped from Bidanur and fled to Bombay, taking with him the entire treasury. It is said that in Bombay, he reconverted to Hinduism.

There are also instances where Tipu cruelly put to death those who were loyal to him for no other reason than mere suspicion. Tipu despised Muhammad Ali, another trusted and loyal lieutenant of Hyder Ali, and had him brutally murdered. The same fate befell an administrative officer named Ghasi Khan Bede, who had earned the goodwill of the citizenry. This was reason enough to invite Tipu's wrath. Ghasi Khan was dismissed from service and then tortured horribly and put to death. And then there was Kasim Khan, a distinguished military leader. He was put in chains, and his hands and nose were chopped off. He later committed suicide.

As William Miles says, this innately paranoid nature of Tipu alienated him from almost everybody including his most trusted minister and confidant Mir Sadiq.

The story that [Tipu] was betrayed by Mir Sadiq...does not appear improbable...As [Tipu] was a great tyrant, there can be no doubt that his ministers were glad to get rid of him on any terms.

Much is made of Mir Sadiq's betrayal of Tipu by modern-day devotees of this savage Sultan. This again is the concoction dished out by Bhagwan S Gidwani who blew up the "betrayal" by Mir Sadiq to catastrophic proportions. However, Mir Sadiq wasn't the only "betrayer." As Miles notes, Tipu's 17-year reign of terror had angered everybody to the point that they decided that he was not worth staying alive. And so in the final battle of 1799, Tipu witnessed hordes of desertions from all quarters.

There was simply no other way it could have ended.

8

Tipu Begins to Chafe Everybody

Almost immediately after he became the king, the Mysore State under Tipu lost direction completely. It seemed as if the throne had shattered whatever remained of an already-temperamental Tipu's mental balance. From the initial days, he began to earn the wrath of everybody. He unleashed a regime of unbridled tyranny in his own dominions, which earned him the distrust and anger of his subjects; nobody, not even the highest officials in his administration and military were spared the fits of his temper. He needlessly provoked and escalated hostilities with his neighbouring Palegars and Nawabs, the Nizam, the Peshwas, and the British.

In fact, it's not far from the truth to say that Tipu's downfall began the moment Hyder Ali died. A good indicator of this is the fact that over his 17-year long rule, Tipu lost more territory than he gained; in fact, he even lost key territories that his father had conquered.

The preface to the first of these losses was written in December 1782 when the British General Mathews arrived from Bombay with a sizeable force and captured the hill-fort of Rajamanadurga at the mouth of the River Mirjan (near Gokarana). After this, he captured Ankola, Sadashivagad, Honnavar, and Mangalore forts. Shortly, he also took the prized fort of Bidanur. It was during this expedition that Ayaz Khan decamped from Bidanur and fled to Bombay taking the entire treasury with him. However, this was not an offensive that the British launched against Tipu. It was a mere diversionary tactic.

Around the time that Mathews was marching towards the coast, Tipu under the orders of his father was stationed in the Malabar, and his large army was a definite threat to Colonel Humberstone who was camped there. However, Humberstone was no match for Tipu's numerically superior force. It was to relieve Humberstone that General Mathews was dispatched. The British tactic worked.

The Treaty of Mangalore

Tipu turned his attention to the coast and reconquered all these forts. He then marched into Bidanur and took it in a breeze—the British troops were a paltry 1600. General Mathews surrendered on the condition that Tipu would allow the British army to return unharmed. However, when he found that Ayaz Khan had emptied the treasury, his fury peaked. He reneged on his promise and imprisoned General Mathews and all his men, placed them in irons and sent them to Srirangapattana. Mathews met a ghastly end. He was made to starve and when he could no longer bear it, begged for food. He was then served poisoned food, which he ate and died.

Next, Tipu turned his attention to the all-important fort of Mangalore, which General Mathews had taken in his triumphant march from Bombay. However, the commandant who was manning the fort had informed Mathews that his hold was untenable given the paucity of troops. Tipu dispatched a small force to recapture the fort but failed. Enraged, he decided to lead the charge personally with a larger force. He sought the help of the French engineers and relentlessly bombarded the fort. His efforts were successful

Tipu battling the British

initially. However, the British Commanding Officer, Colonel Campbell decided to fight back. His courage and valour were exemplary: Tipu's ceaseless attacks had reduced the fort almost to ruins but the British would simply not yield. And then Tipu ran out of luck. The French suddenly refused to support him. The reason: hostilities between the French and the British had ceased in Europe after the Treaty of Versailles was concluded. The entire French contingent on Tipu's side withdrew from the scene of the battle. Tipu now converted the siege into a blockade. Very soon, provisions inside the fort ran out.

The British sued for peace, and Tipu agreed to a temporary armistice. As part of this, the British admiral forbade Colonel Campbell from military engagement. However, Tipu had no intention of honouring the armistice. His objective was to let the British starve to death inside the fort, and he succeeded. Deprived of food and water, the British garrison suffered great distress. Soon, disease broke out, people died, and hospitals were overflowing with sick people. For Tipu, it was *fait accompli*.

The British called for a War Council, which decided that surrender was the best option if the brave garrison had to be saved from total extermination. The Treaty of Mangalore was signed on 11 March 1784 by Governor General Warren Hastings and Tipu Sultan, and was ratified on 20 April 1784.

This treaty is celebrated by self-proclaimed secular historians and other Tipu-worshippers as some sort of a great milestone in Tipu's "fight for freedom." It is indeed a milestone but for all the wrong reasons. This treaty and what Tipu did subsequently are eminent proofs of what he really was. For this reason, it is important to reproduce the full text of the treaty here.

The treaty comprised 10 Articles.

Article 1st.--Peace & friendship shall immediately take place between the said Company the Nabob [Nawab] Tippoo Sultan Bahadur & their friends, and allies, particularly including therein the Rajahs of Tanjore & Travencore, who are friends & allies to the English and the Carnatic Payen Ghaut, also Tippoo Sultan's friends & allies, the Biby of Cannanore, and the Rajahs or Zemindars of the Malabar coast, are included in this treaty, the English will not directly or indirectly assist the enemies of the Nabob Tippoo Sultan Bahadur nor make war upon his friends or allies, and the Nabob Tippoo Sultan Bahadur will not directly or indirectly assist the enemies, nor make war upon the friends or allies of the English.

Article 2nd.--Immediately after signing and sealing the Treaty by the Nabob Tippoo Sultan Bahadur and the three English Commissioners, the said Nabob shall send orders for the complete evacuation of the Carnatic, and the restoration of all the forts and places in it, now possessed by his troops, the forts of Amboorgur and Satgur excepted; & such evacuation and restoration shall actually & effectually be made in the space of thirty days from the day of signing the treaty, and the said Nabob shall also immediately after signing the treaty send orders for the release of all the persons who were taken & made prisoners in the late war, and now alive, whether European or Native, and for their being safely conducted to & delivered at such English Forts or Settlements, as shall be nearest to the places where they now are, so that the said release & delivery of the prisoners shall actually & effectually be made in thirty days from the day of signing the Treaty; the Nabob will cause them to be supplied with provisions and conveyances for the journey, the expense of which shall be made good to him by the Company. The Commissioners will send an officer or officers to accompany the prisoners to the different places, where they are to be delivered, in particular Abdul Wahab Cawn, taken at Chittoor, and his family shall be immediately released, & if willing to return to the Carnatic shall be allowed to do so. If any person or persons belonging to the said Nabob, and taken by the Company in the late war, be now alive, & in prison in Bencoolen, or other territories of the Company such person or persons shall be immediately released, and if willing to return shall be sent without delay to the nearest fort or settlement in the Mysore country. Baswapa, late Amuldar of Palicacherry, shall be released & at liberty to depart.

Article 3rd.--Immediately after signing and sealing the treaty the English Commissioners shall give written orders for the delivery of Onore, Carwar and Sadasewgude, and forts or places adjoining thereto, and send a ship or ships to bring away the Garrisons. The Nabob Tippoo Sultan Bahadur will cause the troops in those places to be supplied with provisions and any other necessary assistance for their voyage to Bombay (they paying for the same). The Commissioners will likewise give at the same time written orders for the immediate delivery of the forts & districts of Caroor, Avaracourchy, & Daraporam; and immediately after the release and delivery of the prisoners, as before mentioned, the fort and district of Dindigul shall be evacuated & restored to the Nabob Tippoo Sultan Bahadur, and none of the troops of the Company shall afterwards remain in the country of the Nabob Tippoo Sultan Bahadur.

Article 4th.--*As soon as all the prisoners are released and delivered, the fort & district of Cananore shall be evacuated and restored to Ali Rajah Biby, the Queen of that country, in the presence of any one person, without troops, whom the Nabob Tippoo Sultan Bahadur may appoint for that purpose, and at the same time that the orders are given, for the evacuation and delivery of the forts of Cananore and Dindigull, the said Nabob shall give written orders for the evacuation, and deliver of Amboorgur and Satgur to the English, and in the meantime none of the troops of the said Nabob shall be left in any part of the Carnatic, except in the two forts above mentioned.*

Article 5th.--*After the conclusion of this treaty the Nabob Tippoo Sultan Bahadur will make no claim whatever in future on the Carnatic.*

Article 6th.--*All persons whatsoever, who have been taken & carried away from the Carnatic Payen Ghaut (which includes Tanjore) by the late Nabob Hyder Ali Cawn Bahadur, who is in heaven, or by the Nabob Tippoo Sultan Bahadur, or otherwise belonging to the Carnatic, and now in the Nabob Tippoo Sultan Bahadur's dominions, and willing to return, shall be immediately allowed to return with their families & children, or as soon as may be convenient to themselves, and all persons belonging to the Vencatagerry Rajah, who were taken prisoners in returning from the fort of Vellour, to which place they had been sent with provisions, shall also be released & permitted immediately to return. Lists of the principal persons belonging to the Nabob Mahomed Ali Cawn Bahadur and to the Rajah of Vencatagherry shall be delivered to the Nabob Tippoo Sultan's ministers, and the Nabob will cause the contents of this article to be publickly notified throughout his country.*

Article 7th.-*This being the happy period of general peace and reconciliation, the Nabob Tippoo Sultan Bahadur as a testimony and proof of his friendship to the English, agrees that the Rajahs or*

Zemindars on this coast, who have favoured the English in the late war shall not be molested on that account.

Article 8th.- *The Nabob Tippoo Sultan Bahadur hereby renews & confirms all the commercial privileges & immunities given to the English by the late Nabob Hyder Ali Cawn Bahadur, who is in heaven, and particularly stipulated & specified in the treaty between the Company, and the said Nabob concluded the 8th of August 1770.*

Article 9th.--*The Nabob Tippoo Sultan Bahadur shall restore the factory and privileges possessed by the English at Callicut until the year 1779 (or 1193 Heggra) and shall restore Mount Dilly & its district, belonging to the settlement of Tellicherry and possessed by the English, till taken by Sadar Cawn, at the commencement of the late war.*

Article 10th.--*This treaty shall be signed and sealed by the English Commissioners and a copy of it shall afterwards be signed & sealed by the President and Select Committee of Fort St. George, and returned to the Nabob Tippoo Sultan Bahadur, in one month, or sooner, if possible, and the same shall be acknowledged under the hands & seals of the Governor General & Council of Bengal, & the Governor & Select Committee of Bombay, as binding upon all the Governments in India, and copies of the treaty, so acknowledged, shall be sent to the said Nabob in three months, or sooner, if possible.*

Tipu recovered all the territory held by Hyder Ali (which had been subsequently wrested by the British) in the Canara and the Malabar regions under this treaty. However, this victory filled Tipu with a sense of invincibility. Puffed up with this, he decided to give a free run to his innate haughtiness and fanaticism. And so, even in a situation of peace, Tipu decided to advertise his Islam-protector credentials to the world. He set his eyes on the Christians on the coast. In his own words:

His Majesty [referring to himself], *the shadow of God, being informed of these circumstances* [of Christians practicing their faith and engaged in proselyting], *the rage of Islam began to boil in his breast. He ordered that an enumeration and description of the houses of all Christians should be made, and then sent detachments under trusty officers who, after early prayers, acting in accordance with their instructions, seized 60,000 (sic) persons, great and small of both sexes, who were carried to the resplendent presence* [Tipu]. *They were then despatched to the capital, and the males being formed into battalions of five hundred each, under the command of officers well instructed in the faith, were honoured with the distinction of Islam, and distributed in the principal garrisons.*

These unfortunate souls were given the honorific, *Ahmadis* or "praiseworthy" and the forcible conversion and conscription was commemorated with the phrase, "God is the protector of the religion of Ahmad." If this wasn't enough, Bowring writes that

Tipu demanded the surrender of the daughters of some of these Christians in order to have them placed in his seraglio, and that, [if the parents refused,] *their noses, ears, and upper lips* [were] *cut off, and were then paraded through the streets on asses, with their faces towards the tails of the animals.*

The Treaty of Mangalore should have taught Tipu at least two valuable lessons. One, his victory owed not to his superior force or strategy but to the tiny British unit, which was in no position to mount an equal opposition. Indeed, Mir Hussain Kirmani, Tipu's sycophant-cum-historian grudgingly praises British heroism:

Colonel Campbell fought with great valour and defended the fort of Mangalore. He did not surrender the fort despite having a shortage of ammunition and supplies, and in the face of an outbreak of disease. Although Tipu's commanders like Hussain Ali fought heroically, they had to retreat after being severely wounded.

A Painting of the Nizam

The second lesson: that Tipu should've woken up to the French who had abandoned him in the thick of the battle. This should have warned him that he couldn't fully rely on them.

On their part, the British had just had a taste of Tipu's double-dealing when he violated the temporary armistice and forced them into surrendering.

But the other South Indian Nawabs and the Nizam had accurately assessed the character of Tipu long ago. Even as the British were engaged with Tipu in Bidanur, the Nawab of Arcot, Muhammad Ali wrote a letter to the British. The subject of the letter was Tipu. This letter dated 7 April 1783 to the Governor General Warren Hastings is quite revealing.

The Nawab of Arcot congratulates the Governor General on the success that attended his wise measures in South India. As a result of the conquest of Bidanur, the troops of Hyder Ali will be totally driven out of the Carnatic. These circumstances together with the ratification of the treaty with the Marathas will enable the English to annihilate the power of Mysore. It was fortunate that Hyder did not live to see his own downfall but died as his power was on the point of extinction. Tipu, his son, now survives to bear the consequences of his cruelty and oppression.

The conquest of Bidanur, and the seaports of that quarter has been possible only through the wise policy and firm action of the Governor General. It has shaken the very foundation of the Government of Mysore, for Bidanur is the key to all the territories over which Hyder had established his sway. Accordingly, it is like a powerful sword in the hands of the Company which will not only serve them in self defence but will also give them a supremacy over all the dominions of this country and enable them to keep the whole of India. The Marathas will be grateful to the English for the restitution of their territory between the Tungabhadra and the Krishna which they had lost to Hyder...When the Raja of Mysore is similarly brought out of his prison and installed on his ancestral [throne], the good name and the sense of justice of the Governor General would spread far and wide. The defence of his country would remain in the hands of his benefactors, that is, the English.

The irony of this request is interesting: here is a Muslim Nawab writing to the British, requesting their help to unseat another Muslim king and install a *Hindu* king in his place.

In a reply on 10 September 1783 to the British response, the Nawab said that he

> *...is convinced of his loyalty and regards* [Warren Hastings] *as one of his sons...he [has] remained faithful to the Governor General as long as he lived. He has rejected the overtures of the French who for a whole month had been soliciting SANADs [Islamic clerics and similar religious authority figures] for the country of Arcot in the name of Hyder Nayak's son and who are offering lakhs of rupees for the consideration.*

One observation clearly stands out in this affair: the Muslim Nawab who was a neighbor was himself terrified and disgusted with Hyder Ali and Tipu's destructive raids and cruelties. His desperation to unseat Tipu was so acute that he passed on intelligence about Tipu's plans and designs to the British, and sought their assistance in restoring the Wodeyar family back to the throne of Mysore. And this was as early as in 1783.

A Treaty-Breaker Embarks on a Spree of Wanton Conquests

It appeared as if the Treaty of Mangalore had suddenly endowed Tipu with an inflated sense of his own prowess. His courtiers at Srirangapattana embarked on an orgy of flattery, glorifying him as this invincible emperor who had brought the British to heel. Tipu took this flattery to be real. He assumed that the Treaty of Mangalore was just a worthless piece of paper and began to violate it almost immediately after it was concluded.

The British had honoured their end of the bargain by returning all the territories they had captured from Tipu. However, on his end, Tipu simply reneged. As part of the treaty, he had to release the British soldiers he had jailed in the hellhole of a prison at Mangalore. However, he massacred all of these British captives including General Matthews, who met a gory end in the prison at Srirangapattana, as narrated earlier. This was just the small beginning of an eight-year saga of flagrant violations of the Treaty of Mangalore that included but was not limited to wanton and barbaric raids against hapless kingdoms and principalities.

In a letter dated 29 May 1784—two months after Tipu had concluded the Treaty of Mangalore—the Nawab of Arcot, Muhammad Ali wrote a letter to the British informing them that

Tipu Sultan has started correspondence with the Sultan of Turkey, and is trying to annex Bijapur to his territories. He has struck coins, both rupees and gold Mohurs [coins], with the figure of an elephant on one side of them, and his name on the other side. [Tipu] wrote to the Nawab Nizam Ali Khan that he [Tipu] was the master of the whole of the country on this side of the River Krishna and that the territories on the other side belonged to the Nawab [Nizam Ali Khan].

Now, Bijapur had historically been part of the Bahamani Sultans, after which it passed on to Mughal hands. Under Aurangzeb, it was a key administrative centre of the Mughal Empire in the South. By all accounts, it was an important power centre in Northern Karnataka because it held strategic importance over the the vast and fertile region between the Tungabhadra and Krishna rivers.

An angry and panicked Nizam sent a 20,000-strong cavalry and infantry under the leadership of his son to meet Tipu. Very soon, he followed this force with a massive army of his own. Meanwhile, the Marathas sent a force from Poona and Satara in response to a request for help from Nizam Ali. When the battle with Nizam Ali occurred at Raichur, Mughal Ali Khan, the brother of the Nizam defected to Tipu's camp. Mughal Ali saw this as an opportunity to settle scores with his brother with whom he had harboured hostilities for long. In the battle that followed, Tipu prevailed and managed to capture a few forts located near the Tungabhadra and Krishna riverbanks. In hindsight, this victory proved useless. Indeed, on the contrary, it exposed Tipu's incompetence as a strategic thinker because in the long term, Tipu had earned the permanent wrath of the formidable Marathas. Lewin Bowring puts it in perspective.

This expedition, though professedly undertaken for the purpose of strengthening his weak northern frontier, implied extraordinary… arrogance on the part of Tipu. He should have known that by provoking a collision with the warlike hosts of the Marathas… he would bring down upon himself a cloud of enemies.

Although useless, this victory only exacerbated Tipu's belief in his own invincibility. He declared himself the *Padshah* (literally, "Master King") after this victory.

However, this was just the beginning. As we shall see, the Marathas, the Nizam, and the Nawab of Arcot did not forget this insult in a hurry. Equally, the British were keenly watching these developments. However, they forgave his numerous and licentious violations of the Mangalore Treaty for eight long years, which was both unnecessary and dangerous. Unnecessary because they had the might and the wherewithal to vanquish him. Dangerous because of what he unleashed in South India during that period.

9

Tipu's Savagery in Coorg

Known as Kodagu in Kannada, Coorg is a picturesque hill-country forming the Southern tip of Karnataka. It forms the border between Karnataka and Kerala, and is in many ways, the gateway to the Malabar region in Kerala. Today, it is primarily known for its scenic beauty and spectacular views of thickly-forested mountain ranges, valleys, waterfalls, and sprawling coffee estates.

Although it is difficult to accurately trace the antiquity of Coorg, we have definite historical records from the 9th Century. Until the British colonization of India, Coorg had always been a principality under powerful dynasties of Karnataka like the Kadambas, Chalukyas, Gangas, Cholas, Rashtrakutas, and the Vijayanagar Empire. The Kodavas (people belonging to Kodagu) had pretty much been a warrior race for much of their existence and often lent their best warriors to fight in battles on behalf of the monarch they owed allegiance to. In fact, this martial heritage is still visible. Thousands of Kodava homes have continued to preserve guns, swords, machetes, and knives of considerable antiquity.

In the 18th Century, Coorg was ruled by a descendant of the Ikkeri Nayakas of Bidanur. When Hyder Ali brutally took over Bidanur in 1763, he decided to annex Coorg as well. In 1765, he sent a considerable force to Coorg but it was easily repelled. Five years later, a succession dispute broke out in

Coorg between Devappa and his uncle Lingaraj. Lingaraj sought Hyder's help, and Hyder, the master schemer was glad that opportunity had itself knocked on his door. He promised to help Lingaraj and marched with a considerable force and reached the capital, Madikeri (or Mercara). Devappa fled but was captured and thrown in the jail at Srirangapattana where he died. However, Hyder did not take Coorg without brutality. According to Lewin Bowring,

> ...on his first appearance on the [Coorg] frontier, Haidar offered a reward of five rupees for the head of every Coorg [Kodava] which was brought to him, and that 700 heads were in consequence delivered.

However, Hyder couldn't hold Coorg for long. A serious insurrection broke out in the region and the capital Madikeri itself was besieged. However, Hyder quickly marched in with a strong force, put down the insurrection and executed every single leader who had led the rebellion. However, even this effort did not last long. Coorg erupted in rebellion yet again.

This time however, Hyder Ali decided to attack it from the South. He dispatched his army via Hunsur. The Kodava army was unable to catch the enemy's scent until it was too late. Hyder's forces had reached Balale near Ponnampet and laid a siege. At night, Hyder's army launched a surprise attack and massacred about 700 Kodavas. Memory of this episode has still been preserved by the local folk legend. However, the Kodava warriors fought back heroically. The details of this battle are mentioned in an inscription at Hunsur. The inscription records how "the black-vest wearing warriors descended upon the enemy like black bees." But then, the outnumbered Kodava soldiers were no match for Hyder Ali's force, which proceeded to hack every Kodava, soldier and citizen alike. When he saw the dismembered head of a beautiful face, Hyder Ali ordered his army to stop the killing. Coorg finally fell into his hands in 1780 in this manner.

However, by the time Tipu assumed power, Coorg was leaderless with all its ruling princes languishing in the Srirangapattana prison. But nothing could shake the courage and the fierce spirit of independence of this proud race. In June 1783, they wrote a letter to a British agent stationed in Srirangapattana requesting protection from Tipu. The letter contained an appeal to the British to send about 6000-7000 men "by the way of Heggala Ghat...in the West, where I would myself join the English troops and fall upon Periyapattana, which place reduced, we could immediately march to Srirangapattana...which would soon be in our possession."

This letter is a testimony to the foresight of the Kodavas, who had accurately estimated the kind of monster that Tipu was and foresaw the horrors that he would unleash. It was signed by one Utha Nayak. To his credit, the British agent James Sibbald, quickly assessed the situation of the Kodavas. Besides, he had already been working on Coorg for some time now, and had sent a detailed report to the Supreme Government of the East India Company in May 1783 describing the immensely strategic value of Coorg. However, the East India Company Government had ignored it for the time being owing to a misplaced sense of honouring the Treaty of Mangalore. As we shall see, Sibbald's report would later prove enormously useful to the British.

The British ignorance proved tragic for the Kodavas in the interim. Indeed, Coorg experienced its worst ever fate and underwent its most humiliating period during Hyder Ali and Tipu Sultan's rule.

Buoyed by the success of the Treaty of Mangalore, Tipu marched into Coorg in 1785 and declared that they were guilty of polyandry. He cautioned them to discard the practice or face the fate of becoming Ahmadis.

Coorg reduced to a wasteland

In 1788, he actually implemented his threat. In a letter to the Nawab of Kurnool Runmust Khan, Tipu gloats about how gloriously he accomplished this vicious task:

...the exciters of sedition in the Coorg country, not looking to the consequences [of such conduct]... raised their heads, one and all, in tumult. Immediately on our hearing of this circumstance, we proceeded with the utmost speed, and, at once, **made prisoners of forty thousand***...Coorgs, who, alarmed at the approach of our victorious army, had slunk into woods, and concealed themselves in lofty mountains, inaccessible even to birds.* **Then carrying them away from their native country we raised them to the honor of Islam, and incorporated them with our Ahmadi corps***. As these happy tidings are calculated, at once, to convey a warning to hypocrites...* (Emphasis added)

There was another angle to Tipu's unprovoked aggression against Coorg.

Among other things, Tipu was obsessed with building overseas ties through trade and diplomacy. However, the British had scuttled him at every step. The British intelligence network was unparalleled, and their tact for building strategic alliances with powerful local kings was equally unmatched. And so, Tipu decided that using the sea route was the best method to accomplish his objective. He found that the Malabar Coast was ideal for this. He hit upon a plan that would give him access to the Malabar Coast. Part of this plan was the complete conquest of Coorg, which connected Mysore to Kerala. Although Hyder Ali had already subdued Coorg, it was still only nominally a feudatory of Mysore.

Tipu marched into Coorg with a large force and launched a savage attack on the pretext of suppressing a rebellion. Indeed, there's some grain of truth about the rebellion, and it has everything to do with a despotic officer named Zein Ul Abiddin Khan. He was Tipu's faithful *Faujdaar* (commander) in Coorg. Here's how Tipu's arch-sycophant cum historian Mir Hussein Kirmani, describes Zein Khan:

The Faujdaar extended the hand of lust to the women of the peasantry, and compelled them to submit to his will and pleasure. In consequence of this tyrannical conduct, the whole of Kodagu advanced into a field of enmity and defiance. The people there rose up in rebellion when Tipu himself entered Kodagu through Periyapattana and Siddapur. He threw himself like a raging lion into the midst of that frightful forest...the Kodagu country...

It's pretty clear that Tipu's objective was to punish the oppressed Kodavas, and not to alleviate their suffering. Equally, it also served as a convenient pretext to achieve his political objective of taking control of the Malabar region.

If Hyder Ali gave a direct fight to the Kodava army, Tipu chose to launch a brutal attack on the most defenceless aspects of the Kodavas—innocent citizens, their way of life, their ancient culture, their religion, and their temples. He hit small towns and villages, often razing them to the ground or burning them down. Instead of battling the Kodava army, he targeted unarmed and innocent citizens. And he attacked, looted and destroyed temples.

Here's Mir Hussein Kirmani again giving us a sample of Tipu's savagery in Coorg.

The conquering Sultan now...dispatched his Amirs and Khans with large bodies of troops to punish those idolaters and reduce the whole country (Coorg) to subjection. Troops under M. Lally...Abbedin [the same tyrannical Faujdaar] and Hussein Ali were sent to Thalakaveri and Kushalpura...attacked and destroyed many towns with 8000 men, women and children taken as prisoners...collected an immense crowd like a flock of sheep or herd of bullocks...while the Sultan pitched his tents to the South of

The Omkareshwara Temple at Madikeri

the Thalakaveri hill...giving them orders to pursue the rebels and capture their chiefs.

Already a thinly-populated country, Tipu's brutal raid followed by large-scale prisoner-taking depopulated Coorg of its original inhabitants. However, that did not seem to bother him. Instead, being the Islamic zealot that he was, Tipu sought to Islamize it with Muslim settlements. He transported about 7000 Muslim families belonging to the Shaikh and Sayyid sects to Coorg from elsewhere.

The intensity of Tipu's raid was so terrifying that hundreds of temple priests fled to Mangalore along with their families. Worship came to a permanent halt in several temples. Some temples were covered with leaves in order to conceal their presence. The Maletirike Bhagavati temple at Virajpet is a good example of this. The Omkareshwara temple in Madikeri—arguably the most well-known temple in

Coorg—faced mortal danger. The ruler at Madikeri realized that Tipu wouldn't spare it and removed the existing tower (Kalasha) of the temple and replaced it with a dome so that it appeared like a mosque from afar. The Omkareshwara temple continues to retain this mosque-like appearance even to this day.

Some historians claim that he killed about 40000 Kodavas and converted an equal number (a fact borne out by his own letter to Runmust Khan). The converted Kodavas were since known as Kodava Mapilas. Also, the fact that there were hundreds of such converted Kodavas in Tipu's Ahmadi unit is a testimony to this historical truth. It also bears repetition that thousands of such captured Kodavas were transported to Ganjam (near Srirangapattana), forcibly converted, and made to join the Ahmadi unit.

Remnants of the savagery that Tipu inflicted upon the hapless Kodavas are visible even today.

In his raid of Napoklu near Madikeri, Tipu destroyed the temples in the surrounding villages of Betu and Kolakeri. He set fire to the house of the Biddatanda family. Forty members of this family were captured as prisoners and transported to Ganjam. After a few years, two members of this family escaped from Ganjam and returned to their hometown. One of them was a warrior named Appanna. However, the people in his hometown decided that he had now become a Mapila (Muslim), and excommunicated him. Appanna built a hut near the town-lake and spent the rest of his life there. This lake was in existence till recently, and was known as the *Appannajja Lake.*

Even today, we find the descendants of these Koda-vas, who were forcibly converted in Tipu's time. These Ko-dava Mapilas till recently used to celebrate native Coorg festivals, built houses (called *ain-mane*) like the non-Muslim

Kodavas, bore the same arms, wore the same kind of jewelry, and carried similar surnames. We have surnames like Alira, Cheeranda, Chimma Cheera (this surname is shared by non-Muslim Kodavas), Duddiyanda, Kaddadiyanda, and Kolumanda in Virajpet. In the Devanageri village, we have Muslim family names like Puliyanda and in the regions surrounding Virajpet, we have Muslim family names like Kuvalera, Italtanda, Mitaltanda, Kuppodanda, Kappanjeera. Similarly, in the Madikeri taluk, we have Kalera, Chekkera, Charmakaranda, Maniyanda, Balasojikaranda, and Mandeyanda. Intriguingly, in the Hoddur village in Madikeri taluk, there is a Muslim family with the surname of Harishchandra!

There's also a curious contemporary fact that has a historical connection to Tipu. Even today, street dogs in Coorg are contemptuously called "Tipu," a measure of how intensely he is reviled theres.

To the Kodavas, Tipu's bigoted dance of death in their homeland remains a wound that will never heal.

10

The Marauder of Malabar

TIPU SULTAN's incursions in the Malabar can form the subject of an independent book. The scale of destruction was unparalleled and the havoc it wreaked—not once but on several occasions—permanently altered the character of entire cities and towns. Like in Coorg, remnants of Tipu's disastrous campaigns in the Malabar can be seen even today in the region. And like Coorg, it was Hyder Ali who had first invaded Malabar, as we have seen earlier in the book.

The Malabar represents the entire region lying between the Western Ghats and the Arabian Sea. The Malabar is also taken to mean the South Western Coast of the Indian Peninsula when it is used in the sense of the "Malabar Coast." Additionally, "Malabar Coast" is also used as an all-encompassing term to include the entire Indian coast beginning at the Konkan to Cape Camorin, the tip of the Indian Peninsula. It is flanked by the Arabian Sea on the West and by the Western Ghats on the East. Today, the Malabar includes all the districts of Northern Kerala—Kasargod, Wayanad, Kannur, Kozhikode, Palakkad, and Malappuram.

Thanks to a long and friendly coastline, the Malabar has held immense significance from time immemorial. It was under the control of the Chera kings till the 12th Century. Following the breakup of the Chera Empire, it passed on, most notably, to the Kolathiris (North Malabar), the Zamorins (Calicut or Kozhikode), and Valluvokonathiris (Walluvanad).

However, from the 13th Century onwards, the Zamorins (or Samuris) of Calicut became all-powerful owing to flourishing international trade. It was on the shores of the Malabar that Vasco Da Gama landed and was received warmly by the Zamorin ruling it then.

Tipu's first foray into the Malabar was under the direction of his father who had ordered him to recapture it. Tipu was near Panniani—in the Malabar—when he received news of Hyder Ali's death near Chittoor.

Tipu looked at the Malabar once again after declaring himself the *Padshah* in the wake of the successes he had obtained against the Marathas, the Nizam, and the Nawab. When he returned to Srirangapattana after this campaign, he ordered the "entire destruction of the old town of Mysore, in order to obliterate all associations with the deposed Rajas."

Calicut razed to the ground

After this, he marched into Calicut and issued a proclamation denouncing the practice of polyandry. He warned the poor Hindus to abandon their ancient social practice failing which he would honour them with Islam. Before departing from Calicut, he appointed a sizeable body of Islamic teachers to keep a watch on these infidels. He entrusted the administration of Malabar to one, Mir Ibrahim who quickly proved to be inept and tyrannical. So tyrannical that within a few months, the Nairs of the Malabar rose up in revolt so fierce that Tipu was compelled to march in person to quell it. And he did quell it with the brutality possible only to him. Here's how Lewin Bowring describes it:

Marching through Coorg with a large army, he sent detachments about the country to hunt down the rebellious Nairs, while he himself proceeded to Kutipuram. Here, two thousand [Nairs] defended themselves and their families with resolution, but were soon obliged to surrender. This gave an opportunity to Tipu to show his apostolic zeal. Orders were issued that the whole of these unfortunates should be offered the alternative of becoming good Musalmans, or, in case of noncompliance, that they should be banished to [Srirangapattana]. They reluctantly acquiesced in the former alternative, knowing well what the deportation meant. The next day, accordingly, all the males were circumcised, while both sexes were compelled to eat beef, as a proof of their conversion. One of the principal victims of Tipu's revenge was the Raja of Chirakkal, of ancient descent, who, having been falsely accused of conspiring, was attacked and killed, and his body hung up after his death. In this raid the Mysore sovereign is said to have carried off large treasures plundered from the temples in Malabar. He crowned his achievements by compelling the princess of Cannanore to marry her daughter to his son, Abd-ul-Khalik.

Copious amounts of first hand testimony to Tipu's atrocities in Calicut exist, and all of them unanimously hold that Tipu razed the entire city to the ground in the most brutal manner. Notable accounts include William Logan's *Malabar Manual*, the *Malabar Gazetter*, Portuguese missionary Fr. Bartholomew's *Voyage to East Indies*, the German missionary Guntest, and accounts by various contemporary British military officers. A short but vivid sample from Fr. Bartholomew's account will suffice to illustrate the nature of Tipu's raid:

First a corps of 30,000 barbarians who butchered everybody on the way... followed by the field-gun unit... Tipu was riding on an elephant behind which another army of 30,000 soldiers followed. Most of the men and women were hanged in Calicut, first mothers were hanged with their children tied to necks of mothers. That barbarian Tipu Sultan tied the naked Christians and Hindus to the legs of elephants and made the elephants to move around till the bodies of the helpless victims were torn to pieces. Temples and churches were ordered to be burned down, desecrated and destroyed.

Christian and Hindu women were forced to marry Mohammadans and similarly their men were forced to marry Mohammadan women.1 Those Christians who refused to be honoured with Islam, were ordered to be killed by hanging immediately. These atrocities were told to me by the victims of Tipu Sultan who escaped from the clutches of his army and reached Varappuzha, which is the centre of Carmichael Christian Mission. I myself helped many victims to cross the Varappuzha river by boats.

Indeed, the devastation in Calicut was so comprehensive that it changed the character of the place forever. Calicut was home to more than 7000 Brahmin families. Thanks to Tipu, more than 2000 of these were wiped out, and the remaining fled to the forests. In the words of the German missionary Guntest, "Accompanied by an army of 60,000, Tipu Sultan came to Kozhikode [Calicut] in 1788 and razed it to the ground. It is not possible even to describe the brutalities committed by that Islamic barbarian from *Mysore.*"

Tipu himself celebrates this dance of death in Calicut in letters written to various officers under his command. In a letter to Syed Abdul Dulai he gloats that

With the grace of Prophet Mohammed and Allah, almost all Hindus in Calicut are converted to Islam. Only on the borders of Cochin State a few are still not converted. I am determined to convert them also very soon. I consider this as Jehad to achieve that object.

Here is another letter commending his officer Budruz Zuman Khan thus:

Your two letters, with the enclosed memorandums of the Naimar (or Nair) captives, have been received. You did right in ordering a hundred and thirty-five of them to be circumcised, and in putting eleven of the youngest of these into the Usud Ilhye band (or class) and the remaining ninety-four into the Ahmedy Troop...

In yet another letter to the selfsame Budruz Khan, Tipu celebrates the triumph of his fanaticism in a different way:

I have achieved a great victory recently in Malabar and over four lakh Hindus were converted to Islam. I am now determined to march against the cursed Raman Nair.

Tipu beaten twice by the Nair army

This Raman Nair was also known as the Dharma Raja of Travancore. As we've seen in the account of Tipu's barbarism in Coorg, Tipu longed to capture the entire Malabar region so he could possess strategic advantage over the British. He was merely looking for a pretext to launch a raid and he found it in the Travancore Raja. According to Tipu, the Travancore Raja had committed two unforgivable blunders—the first, of erecting defences in the territory of the Cochin Raja who was Tipu's feudatory, and the second, of purchasing the forts of Kranganur and Ayakota from the Dutch.

And so, Tipu approached the Cochin Raja for help in the planned attack against Travancore. Although his feudatory, the Cochin Raja had by now realized the kind of fanatical monster that Tipu was, and gave evasive replies. Indeed, most Rajas and chieftains of Kerala had developed a singular aversion for and dread of Tipu owing to his extremely barbaric nature of mass killings and forcible conversions of Hindus and his large scale temple destructions.

Undeterred, Tipu marched into Travancore and hit the defences that the Raja had erected. He paid no heed to the objections of the Travancore Raja as well as that of the British Government in Madras (to which Travancore owed allegiance). However, as Tipu discovered, the Raja was no pushover. His small but ferocious Nair army routed Tipu's force conclusively to the extent that Tipu himself had to flee for life! Lewin Bowring's description of the battle makes for compulsive reading:

On December 28, 1789, Tipu's army, under his personal command, appeared before the walls, his force consisting of 14,000 infantry and 500 pioneers. By daybreak of the 29th, his troops had gained an entrance and taken possession of a part of the ramparts to the right, the Travancore soldiers contesting each post, but being compelled to retreat before the enemy till they were forced back upon a strong position where, with the aid of a small gun, they made a stand. Fresh troops were ordered up by Tipu to carry the building, and support the leading corps. But the movement was clumsily performed, and in the confusion which ensued, a small body of the defenders, who were posted in a thick cover close to the ramparts, threw in such a heavy fire' that the assailants were repulsed, and a panic ensued. The whole of Tipu's army was soon in precipitate flight, he himself being earned away by the rush. The ditch was filled with the bodies of those who were forced on from behind and trampled underfoot before they could extricate themselves. The bearers of Tipu's palankeen [palanquin] were among the fallen, and he himself escaped with the greatest difficulty, through the exertions of some faithful servants, but lamed in the efforts he had made to save himself. In the hurly-burly he lost his sword and shield, which were taken away in triumph to Trivandrum, the capital of Travancore. He is said to have lost no less than 2,000 men in this miserable affair.

Indeed, in a rare glimpse of honesty, that arch Tipu-sycophant Mir Kirmani concedes how his master was beaten:

The enemy attacked the Sultan's troops on all sides with arrows and musketry, and caused incalculable distress and confusion among them...about 400 brave horsemen...were killed and wounded in front of the Sultan. At this time, Kamaruddin Khan...took [the Sultan] out of his palanquin...and carried through the water to the opposite side of the river...But of those present in that battle, not one man ever returned safe...The Sultan's palanquin with its bed, the great seal of the exchequer and a dagger were taken by the infidels.

In the end, the Raja of Travancore lost the war. His force was no match for Tipu's superior numbers as well as the kind of weaponry he possessed. Yet, he took more than a month to finally break the Travancore fortifications and gain total victory. And then it was same story of despoliation, death, destruction, and plunder. We can turn to Bowring again:

The Mysore army, flushed with success, now began to lay waste the country with fire and sword, desecrating and despoiling temples, and burning towns and villages, whose wretched inhabitants fled to the hills, where many were seized and made prisoners. The ruins to be seen at the present day testify to the ferocity of the invaders, while all the records of antiquity and the archives of the Travancore State were consumed in the burning pagodas, public offices, and houses. These atrocities were perpetrated with the express sanction of Tipu Sultan, who himself marched with his main army southward to Alwal, a favourite watering-place of the Travancore Raja. He contemplated the reduction of the whole province.

And yet, Tipu's success was short-lived. As he pressed forward, taking more territories of Travancore, he was met with the forces of the Travancore Raja's Diwan, Keshava Pillai. This foresighted Diwan had strengthened the main garrisons, and constructed stockades all along the various backwater passages. These measures had the desired impact: the slowing down of Tipu's progress. And then monsoon struck. The whole area was inundated with severe floods and boats became the only means of travel. Meanwhile, Tipu also got wind of the fact that the British had assembled an army at Tiruchinapalli. With no other option, he beat a hasty retreat to Palghat, losing a lot of his men en route.

This was Tipu's *second* defeat at the hands of the brave Nairs in reasonably short span of time putting to rest the other lie that agenda-pushing historians of our time spout: that Tipu was this undefeated, fierce warrior who the British greatly feared.

The Malabar devastated

In this context, it's also pertinent to mention a 1964 book published by the Pakistan Administrative Staff College at Lahore. Entitled *Life of Tipu Sultan*, this book summarizes Tipu's destructive raid in the Malabar as follows:

Tipu imprisoned and forcibly converted more than a lakh Hindus and over 70,000 Christians in the Malabar region (they were forcibly circumcised and made to eat beef). Although these conversions were unethical and disgraceful, they served Tipu's purpose. Once all these people had been cut off from their original faith, they were left with no option but to accept the very faith to which their ravager belonged, and they began to educate their children in Islam. They were later enlisted in the army and received good positions. Most of them morphed into religious zealots, and enhanced the ranks of the Faithful in Tipu's kingdom. Tipu's zeal for conversion was not limited only to the Malabar region. He had spread it all the way up to Coimbatore. But for the remonstrance of his mother, Tipu would have compelled his favourite Dewan Poornayya to have forsaken the religion of his forefathers.

This, in a book written by an official organ of the Pakistani Government.

Even a summary of Tipu's atrocities in the Malabar makes for painful reading. Colonel Fullerton's report on the matter is one such account. During his 1783 siege of the Palaghat fort,

Tipu's soldiers daily exposed the heads of many innocent Brahmins within sight from the fort for Zamorin and his Hindu followers to see. It is asserted that the Zamorin rather than witness such enormities and to avoid further killing of innocent Brahmins, chose to abandon the Palghat Fort.

In fact, it is not inaccurate to say that Tipu's (later) Malabar campaign was—apart from trying to secure strategic advantage—a campaign motivated by extreme religious fanaticism against the Hindus of Kerala. Tipu and his army spared no section of the Hindu society—Brahmins, Nairs, Thiyyas, Christians, women, and children. Fullerton continues,

It was not only against the Brahmins who were thus put in a state of terror of forcible circumcision and conversion; but against all sections of Hindus. In August, 1788, a Raja of the Kshatriya family of Parappanad and also Trichera Thiruppad, a chieftain of Nilamboor, and many other Hindu nobles who had been carried away earlier to Coimbatore by Tipu Sultan, were forcibly circumcised and forced to cat beef. Nairs in desperation, under the circumstances, rose up against their Muslim oppressors under Tipu's command in South Malabar and the Hindus of Coorg in the North also joined them...

A Sreedhara Menon, the former editor of the *Gazetteer of Kerala* mentions that

Hindus, especially Nairs and chieftains who resisted Islamic cruelties, were the main targets of Tipu's anger. Hundreds of Nair women and children were abducted to Sreerangapatanam or sold as slaves to the Dutch. Nairs were hunted down and killed and also deprived of all traditional and social privileges. Thousands of Brahmins, Kshatriyas, Nairs and other respected classes of Hindus were forcibly converted to Islam or driven out of their traditional ancestral homes. Thousands sought refuge in Travancore State while hundreds fled to forests and hills to escape Tipu's atrocities which had completely shaken their sense of security.

The new phase of Mysore administration in Kerala resulted in unending wars. Extreme cruelties of the invading army had badly affected every section of the society, leading to the mass exodus of people from Malabar.

Many Hindu temples, royal houses and chieftain families were destroyed and plundered. The exodus of Brahmins and Kshatriyas

TIPU SULTAN: The Tyrant of Mysore

who were the patrons and custodians of traditional arts and culture, resulted in stagnation in the cultural field also.

And it wasn't limited to just this. The consequence of Tipu's overwhelming savagery in the Malabar was all-encompassing. Until then, the Malabar region was renowned for its flourishing pepper and spice trade. However, when Tipu burnt and destroyed several cities and towns in one disastrous sweep, this trade was killed almost overnight. If this wasn't enough, Tipu followed it up by imposing an extortionate tax regime, which in turn forced the peasants to flee to the mountains and forests. Pepper cultivation stopped. Foreign trade was obliterated. People fell into destitution.

No encomium is enough to praise the guts and courage of the Nairs who at great cost fought this bigot. The initial round of rebellion was led by Raja Ravi Varma hailing from the Zamorin lineage. He successfully helped more than 30,000 Brahmins to migrate from Calicut to Travancore. This apart, he assisted a large number of women and men from major and minor royal families—Punnathoor, Nilamboor, Kavalapara, Azhvancherry and Thamprakkal—to flee to Travancore. These families then made Travancore their permanent home after they heard how Tipu had razed Calicut to the ground. Their fear of Tipu too, was permanent. One consequence was the near-drastic change in the demographics of Calicut.

Even more telling are the first-hand accounts left behind by these royal families. These taken together with the *Malabar Manual* reveal the fact that about half the population of Kerala's Hindus fled to the forests of Tellicherry and Travancore. Even the powerful Cochin royal family escaped to the Vaikkom Palace when it heard that Tipu had reached Alwaye.

Other evidence of Tipu's barbarism in the Malabar has survived even today. In the words of the scholar and researcher Ravi Varma,

One finds a heavy concentration of Mappilas [Kerala/Malabar Muslims] *along the invasion routes of Tipu's army, including the places of its temporary occupation, as in Mangalore, Cannanoor, Ponnani, Kondotty, Malappuram, Calicut, Kodungallur, Chawakat, Alwaye, Coimbatore, and Dindigal. This is another proof of forcible circumcision and conversion of helpless Nairs, defenceless Thiyyas and poor Cherumans on a mass scale. Even today, the origin of many Kshatriya, Nair and Brahmin families settled in Travancore and Cochin can be traced back to their ancestral families in Malabar - yet another proof of the severity of Tipu's atrocities against Hindus during his Islamic wars in Kerala.*

Indeed, some regions of Kerala regard Hyder Ali and Tipu Sultan's incursions into their land as the darkest chapter of their history. Even today, the people of the Malabar recall Tipu's brutal campaign with one word that has dark and painful connotations for them: *padayottam* (military campaign).

In hindsight, the British must also share some blame in this sordid affair. Perhaps it was a sense of misplaced generosity, perhaps they took honouring a treaty to the extreme, or perhaps it was the incompetence and/or corruption of the bureaucrats at Madras, or perhaps it was a combination of all these. One of the clauses of the Treaty of Mangalore was the fact that the British would cede complete control of the Malabar to Tipu. To a bigoted Muslim and a habitual word-breaker like Tipu, this only meant one thing—that he could do as he pleased. As we've seen, Tipu had begun to violate the Treaty of Mangalore from day one. But what surprises us is the kind of patience the British displayed even as Tipu went on violating it with grand abandon. What also surprises us is how the British became deaf to the urgent pleas for help from the various Rajas of Kerala—chiefly the Rajas of Cochin and Travancore—who were British allies. One explanation is advanced for this by Ravi Varma.

...the then Governor of Madras, Mr. Holland, in spite of the obligations under the Treaty of Mangalore, specifically instructed the British contingents sent to the Travancore borders, not to assist the Travancore forces in case of war. When the Governor General, Lord Cornwallis, heard about Travancore's victory over Tipu's forces, he assumed at first that it was due to the active assistance rendered by the English Company. But later on, he came to know about the dubious actions and the corrupt character of Mr. Holland. The Governor of Madras was believed to be in the pay of Tipu Sultan. So he was relieved of his responsibilities and Lord Cornwallis himself assumed command of the Madras Army.

A little too late. By the time Cornwallis took charge, hundreds of thousands of unfortunate Hindus of Kerala had already been butchered, deported, and forcibly converted.

11

A Temple Destroyer Par Excellence

One of the most characteristic features of almost all medieval Muslim invaders and rulers of India is their religion-fuelled zeal for destroying Hindu temples. From Muhammad Ghaznavid to Babur to Malik Kafur to Muhammad Bin Tughlaq to Aurangzeb to Nadir Shah, every single Muslim invader and/or ruler made temple destruction his mandatory religious duty. In this, Tipu Sultan stands shoulder-to-shoulder with these temple destroyers extraordinaire.

The record of Tipu Sultan's temple destruction in South India is perhaps best summed up by B. Lewis Rice, the eminent British epigraphist and director of the Archaeology Department of the British Government:

*In the vast empire of Tipu Sultan on the eve of his death, there were only **two** Hindu temples having daily pujas within the Sreerangapatanam fortress. It is only for the satisfaction of the Brahmin astrologers who used to study his horoscope that Tipu Sultan had spared those two temples. The entire wealth of every Hindu temple was confiscated before 1790 itself mainly to make up for the revenue loss due to total prohibition in the country.* [Emphasis added]

Destruction of Hindu temples and idols—apart from the genocide and forcible conversions of Hindus and Christians—formed an inseparable part of Tipu's sprees of wanton aggression from 1783-89 in Coorg and the Malabar.

The Lahore Staff College publication on Tipu recounts his official edict to destroy Hindu temples in his dominions as follows:

He [Tipu] issued an edict for the destruction of all the Hindu temples in his dominions excepting those of Srirangapattana and Melukote...he resolved to destroy every monument of the former Government to which end he caused the ancient fort and city of Mysore to be razed, and removed the stones of the temples and palace to a neighboring hill where he laid the foundation of a new fort which he named Nuzerbad. But in the furiousness of his wrath, he spared not the works of the greatest public utility, in the destruction of the celebrated reservoir of Yadavi Nudi because it recorded the wisdom, riches and power of the ancient Hindu sovereigns. (Emphasis added)

To get a measure of the kind of large scale temple destruction that Tipu carried out, one only needs to peruse William Logan's *Malabar Manual*, which gives a near-complete list of all the temples he had destroyed. More on this a little later.

Lewis Rice estimates in his *Mysore Gazetteer* that Tipu had destroyed about 8000 temples in South India. Colonel R.D. Palsokar also confirms this number in his study on Tipu Sultan when he says that

Tipu relates that he had destroyed 8000 temples, many of them with roofs of gold, silver, copper and all containing treasures buried under the idols. The Raja of Cherakal offered him Rs. 400000 and the plates of gold with which one particular temple was roofed but Tipu said that he would not spare it for all the treasures of the earth and sea.

Indeed, Tipu's refusal to spare the temple in exchange for money reminds us of that arch-iconoclast, Muhmmad Ghaznavid who responded thus when he was made a similar offer:

I desire that on the day of resurrection I should be summoned with the words 'Where is that Mahmud who broke the greatest of heathen idols?' rather than by these: 'Where is that Mahmud who sold the greatest of the idols to the infidels for gold?'

As numerous works of medieval Indian history show, rulers like Muhammad Ghaznavid, Aurangzeb, Tipu *et al* regarded their acts of temple destruction as a pious performance in the service of Islam. Even today, we see a mosque in Srirangapattana—not far from the ruins of Tipu's fort—that was raised after destroying a Hanuman temple. The mosque has no characterstics of a typical mosque except its dome and minaret. The plan and structure of the ramparts and vast compound display unmistakably, the architecture of a Hindu temple. The pillars of this mosque show friezes of Hindu gods carved onto them.

Although the Malabar region bore the brunt of Tipu's temple destruction, its sorry fate was shared by other places as well. Colonel Fullerton was serving in the British army, which was rendering assistance to the Rajas of the Malabar and petty chieftains in Tamil Nadu. Some of his observations and experiences have been recorded in Colonel Castell's *History of India.* Colonel Fullerton's report to his superiors with respect to his unit's battle with Tipu is very revealing.

There a very steep fort at a town near Coimbatore. Near it was a Shiva temple made entirely of black stone. Tipu fell upon this temple which contained beautiful Hindu sculptures, destroyed it completely, and looted all the gold, ornaments, and valuables in it.

Tipu's attack was so savage that the local kings were terrified into not putting up a resistance. It was only after the British arrived there that these kings narrated their woes. Fullerton continues:

This temple was extremely sacred to the Hindus. Tipu had despoiled this temple so badly that it had greatly enraged the Hindus. Until then, nobody had done an iota of harm to the temple.

Tipu's industrial-scale temple destruction in the Malabar

The *Malabar Manual* mentions that the Thrichambaram and Thalipparampu temples in Chirackal Taluqa, Thiruvangatu Temple (Brass Pagoda) in Tellicherry, and Ponmeri Temple near Badakara were destroyed by Tipu Sultan. Equally, the Maniyoor mosque was built after razing a Hindu temple to the ground. Vatakkankoor Raja Raja Varma's *History of Sanskrit Literature* echoes Logan's *Malabar Manual* more vividly:

There was no limit as to the loss the Hindu temples suffered due to the military operations of Tipu Sultan. Burning down the temples, destruction of the idols installed therein and also cutting the heads of cattle over the temple deities were the cruel entertainments of Tipu Sultan and his equally cruel army. It was heartrending even to imagine the destruction caused by Tipu Sultan in the famous ancient temples of Thalipparampu and Thrichambaram. The devastation caused by this new Ravana's barbarous activities has not yet been fully rectified.

The following is a partial list of the important temples that Tipu destroyed in the Malabar region.

Temples Destroyed	Region
Thali, Thiruvannur, Varackal, Puthur, Govindapuram, Thalikkunnu	Calicut
Keraladheeswaram, Thrikkandiyoor, Thriprangatu	Vettum
Tirunavaya	Malappuram
Thrikkavu	Ponnani
Kotikkunnu, Thrithala, Panniyoor, Sukapuram	Kannur, Malappuram
Perumparampu, Maranelira	Edappadu

Vengari, Thrikkulam	Eranadu
Azhinjillam	Ramanattukara
Indyannur, Mannur	Kannur
Mammiyoor	Guruvayoor
Guruvayoor (Krishna Temple)	Guruvayoor
Parampathali, Panmayanadu, Vengidangu	Guruvayoor
Kalpathi, Kachamkurissi	Palghat (Palakkad)
Perumanam	Thrissur
Irinjalakuda, Thiruvanchikulam	Irinjalakuda
Vadakhumnnathan	Thrissur
Shiva Temple	Belur
Jain Temple	Palghat
Vengara Temple	Aranadu
Vadukunda Siva Temple	Madai
Triprangot, Thrichembaram, Thirunavaya, Thiruvannoor, Calicut Thali, Venkitangu, Terumanam, Shri Veliyanattukava, Varakkal, Puthu, Govindapuram, Maranehei Temple of Aaalvancheiri Tambrakkal, Tikulam, Ramanathakra, Azhinjalam Indiannur, Mannur Narayan Kanniar	Various

It is also pertinent to mention the fate that certain renowned temples met at the hands of this Marauder of Malabar.

The Thirunavaya Temple, of unknown antiquity—local legends trace it back to about 5000 years but its written history dates to at least 1300 years—is today located 12 Kilometres south of Tirur in the Malappuram district. It was always renowned as one of the great centres of Vedic learning and a principal place of pilgrimage of the Vaishnava sect. Tipu's brutal army not only plundered the temple but desecrated and destroyed it.

The case of the Thrikkavu temple in Ponnani was no different. After smashing the idols in the temple, Tipu converted the entire temple into an ammunition depot.

Tipu also didn't spare the Krishna temple at Guruvayoor, which is one of the holiest Hindu temples in India. However, today's Tipu-worshippers assert that it was Tipu who gave the land grant to Hindus to construct the Guruvayoor temple! An eminence named C.K. Ahmed writes with supreme confidence that "the Guruvayoor temple of today exists on the land that was granted as *Inaam* [gift or grant] by Tipu" but fails to give a single shred of evidence to back his assertion. However, the real story is that when the people of Guruvayoor heard of Tipu's approach, they secretly transported its main idol to the Ambalapuzha Krishna temple then in the Travancore State. Here's what the 2 January 1977 issue of the *Illustrated Weekly of India* says about the affair:

The truth is that when Tipu raided the Malabar, he looted all the gold and jewelry in the Hindu temples there, pulled down the gold, silver and copper covering that placed on the roofs of these temples, looted their money, and vandalized them. Seeing the nature of his raid, the locals and Brahmins at Guruvayoor feared for the fate of the idol of Krishna in the temple, shifted it to Ambalapuzha and hid it.

It was only after Tipu's tyrannical regime ended that the original idol of Krishna was transported back to Guruvayoor and reinstated with due ceremony. Equally, if no signs of destruction are visible today, it is because of the intervention of an officer named Hydrose Kutty, a Hindu who had been forcibly converted to Islam by Hyder Ali. He helped repair, renovate, and restore the temple and reinstated the land grants and exemptions that had historically been given to it by various kings.

However, the bigoted handwork of Tipu is clearly visible even today in the temples of Parampathali, Panmayanadu and Vengidangu. One look at the appalling damage done to the sanctum sanctorum of the Parampathali temple is sufficient to estimate the nature of Tipu's iconoclasm.

12

Tipu's Luck Begins to Run Out

It is impossible to get a perspective on Tipu Sultan's career and regime without examining the role that the French played in his affairs.

Both Hyder Ali's army and administration boasted of a significant presence of Frenchmen. None of these Frenchmen—both under Hyder and later, Tipu—reported to or drew their salaries from the French Government. Hyder Ali had specifically sought out French soldiers, senior military leaders, strategists and engineers, and employed them at handsome salaries. And Tipu not only continued this practice of his father but embellished it as part of his grand strategy against the British. The results were predictably disastrous because the French were never a dependable ally either to Hyder or Tipu from the start.

The French allied with Tipu for two important reasons. The first was obviously the generous salaries he gave them, and the second, to manipulate him to achieve their own ends—one main objective was to use Tipu as a countervailing force against the British. As we saw earlier, this hope was dashed after the Treaty of Versailles was signed. After this, the French gradually abandoned any hopes of becoming a dominant player in India.

When it was confirmed that Hyder Ali was on his deathbed, senior French officers in his service had already gained an accurate estimate of Tipu's character. They knew that he was essentially a megalomaniac who was also suffused with incurable religious fanaticism. They were also aware that he had no vision and lacked any administrative competence. And so they resorted to flattery and intrigue to great effect. The role of the French in ensuring Tipu's ascension to the throne was significant. However, they never took Tipu seriously from the first to the last. They treated him with exaggerated respect and their assurance of assistance was mere lip service.

Forget Tipu, the French didn't reciprocate Hyder Ali's overtures in the same degree. In Lewin Bowring's succinct assessment, Hyder Ali's

> *want of success was mainly due to the supineness of the French Government, which reserved all its strength for its operations against [British] in North America, and seemed quite indifferent to recovering the prestige it had lost in India.* **Had it despatched a sufficient army to the Coromandel coast when Haidar was operating against the Madras forces, there can be little doubt that Fort St. George would have fallen, and that the British authority would have been supplanted by the French flag.** *De Bussy arrived too late, and with Haidar's death, and the success of [Warren] Hastings' diplomacy, commenced the final decline of French influence in India.* (Emphasis added)

In September 1783, the French General D. Bussy wrote a letter to the Mughal emperor Shah Alam. The letter dispatched through the Nawab of Arcot read as follows:

> *...[Bussy's] master, the King of France has appointed him [Bussy] Commander-in-Chief of all his land and sea forces on account of the absolute trust he reposes in him. He has received from Col. Demonte a copy of the letter sent to him by his Majesty [Shah Alam] desiring him to bring out a reinforcement of French troops who in conjunction with the royal forces may annihilate the*

English power in India. He assures his Majesty that he will fight for him with all his might; Also received orders from his master, the King of France, to proceed to India at the head of 10,000 European soldiers and twenty ships in order to wipe off the British from that land and restore it to its lawful masters.

....He has now arrived in India and is preparing to launch his campaign. He will inform his majesty [Shah Alam] when he commences operation, and begs that his Majesty will not lend ear to any representations of the English whose perfidy, tyranny and usurpations are well-known to him. He is convinced that if His Majesty's forces unite with the French, they will completely frustrate the designs of the English to bring the whole country under their sway. Col. Demonte has been commissioned to negotiate the terms with His Majesty's ministers.

Another important item mentioned in this letter is the fact that the French had made an effort to instigate various Muslim nawabs and chieftains against the British. However, the Nawab of Arcot who was chosen to deliver this letter to the Mughal emperor simply passed it on to the British! It is impossible to believe that the French were naïve enough to *not* realize the implications of routing this letter through the Arcot Nawab whose aversion and hatred for Tipu was well-known.

An incompetent strategist

Neither did Tipu learn anything from the desertion of the French during the siege of the Mangalore fort. And that desertion was just a tiny fraction in a series of let-downs by the French.

Then there was yet the all-important reason for why everything that Tipu touched turned to dust. This reason lies in a fatal flaw of his character: an unshakeable belief in his own invincibility, which was perhaps the biggest reason that prevented him from even admitting the possibility that his enemies were far shrewder and powerful than him. It was this belief that made him assume that he was a master strategist. A few examples of his strategic thinking will suffice to show how ridiculous he ended up looking.

In a bid to cozy up to the Marathas, he wrote to them,

You must realize that I am not at all your enemy. Your enemy is the Englishman of whom you should beware.

In letters to Muslim rulers, he abused the Marathas addressing them as "those worthless Sardars of the Poona infidels." Here is a representative letter addressed to Zaman Shah of Kabul:

Your Majesty would soon proceed...to prosecute a holy war against the infidels...should those infidel Brahmins [Marathas] direct their power...the hands of the heroes of the Faith [Muslim soldiers] in this part of the world shall be raised for their chastisement. We should unite in carrying on a holy war against the infidels...Delhi, the seat of the Government of the Muhammadan faith has been reduced to this state of ruin so that the infidels altogether prevail...we should unite in carrying a holy war against the infidels and free these regions of Hindustan.

He wrote similar letters to the Arcot Nawab and the Nizam urging them to unite under the banner of Islam and help him in his holy war against the British and the infidel Hindus. And then, not to mention, the Treaty of Mangalore which he began to violate almost immediately.

In hindsight, it appears quite incredible that Tipu did all this assuming that nobody would notice that he was playing all sides. Indeed, there's a grain of truth to that. Tipu was hugely lucky in one significant respect: the British inaction for about six long years. He mistook it to mean that the British were scared of him.

Tipu amasses enemies

The 1783-89 era witnessed Tipu's blitzkrieg of deliberately provocative and aggressive campaigns. Already a fanatical Muslim, Tipu's zealotry was exacerbated by his innately vicious nature. It was this that made him wrest the territories of the Nawabs of Arcot and Kurnool even when they had not provoked him. In the raid on the fort of Imitiazgur, "one of the strongest in the entire Hindustan," Tipu extracted a tribute that would fill the granaries of Srirangapattana with "crop provisions sufficient for the consumption of one lakh men for one year."

In 1785, he raided and captured Adoni, a principality that belonged to Mahabat Jung, the Nizam's nephew. Worse, his siege of the Adoni fort came with the unspoken threat of what he would do to the women and children inside the fort. Mahabat Jung had to remove them to safety with great difficulty. The Adoni raid immensely enraged all Muslims in South India.

In 1786 and 1787, he raided several other districts including Periyapattana, Coorg, Belur, and Manjarabad (Sakaleshpur). However, his crossing of the Tungabhadra River and his capture of Badami in 1786 proved decisive. Once this was accomplished, he easily took Bijapur and Ahmednagar. After this, he conquered the border districts like Kanakagiri, Anegondi, Savanur, Rayadurga, and Harapanahalli.

Later, Tipu turned towards the northern border of Mysore. The Palegar of Sondoor had died and his wife Tungamma was in charge of the principality. Tipu vowed to subdue her but she escaped and crossed the Tungabhadra River. Her 12-year old son was left behind and the unfortunate lad was captured, converted, and given the name of Ali Murdan Khan. He was then married off to the daughter of

Khan Jehan, who was originally a Brahmin belonging to the Deshpande family from Kolar. M. Lally led this expedition to Sondoor.

Of course, we've already seen his savagery in Coorg and the Malabar. In passing, it is worth recounting this note by the Pakistan Administrative Staff College's publication on Tipu:

[Tipu] nominated his generals, M.Lally (a Frenchman) Hussein Ali Khan, Mir Muhammad and Imaam Khan to attach their towns and forts....in...eight months, some 80,000 men and women were made prisoners with several chiefs and many of their strongholds and towns reduced. The Raja of Kodagu (Coorg) after a captivity of four years effected his escape. Shortly afterwards, Mamutti Nair died, and Ranga Nair became a convert to Islam with the rest of the captives; he was named Sheikh Muhammad, and...the above captive proselytes were placed under him.

An important fact stands out in all these wanton raids of Tipu, which were accompanied by description-defying brutalities: he did not fight a *single* battle against the British during those six years. All his campagins were directed at tiny principalities, and weak and powerless Palegars and chieftains. Needless, his wars against the Nizam and the Marathas were acts of unprovoked aggression on his part. And there was the record of his savageries.

And so as Tipu went on a rampage on one side, the list of his enemies began to grow longer on the other side. By 1789, he had managed to earn the wrath of every single Raja, Nawab, and chieftain in South India. And all of these rulers were in one way or the other, the allies of the British. Even worse, Tipu's own feudatories, governors, ministers, and officials in the administration were sharpening their knives against him. This is a measure of the extent of his extreme religious fanaticism and unbridled tyranny.

And these aggrieved parties had pleaded with the British to rein in this "barbarian from Mysore" without success. When these pleas became more fervent and came from numerous quarters, the British began to take notice. And then there was the all-important issue of Tipu's serial violations of the Treaty of Mangalore, which these aggrieved parties mentioned. Also, by now, Tipu's brutalities had breached all limits of tolerance.

The British's misplaced fealty to the Treaty of Mangalore for six years holds an important lesson. Today, all those eminences who proclaim from rooftops that Tipu declared war against the British in order to drive them out of India, in order to liberate India from British slavery and similar untruths conveniently suppress an important fact: *Tipu did not fight a single battle against the British after the battle at Mangalore!*

And so, by 1789, the cup of Tipu's sins was filled to the brim. The time had arrived when he had to pay the wages of those sins.

13

Tipu's Enemies Unite and Delegate the Leadership to the British

T
ipu's savage attack on Travancore in 1789 finally tipped the scales against him. In the words of Bowring:

Cornwallis... had foreseen that hostilities were inevitable, and that the half-measures of the Madras authorities had only increased the pride and presumption of the Mysore potentate. So far, however, he had contented himself with warnings and remonstrances, but the unprovoked attack of Tipu on the Travancore State decided him to take active steps to put a stop to further aggressions on allies of the British.

Cornwallis entered into a "treaty of offensive and defensive alliance" with the Marathas and the Nizam. He appointed General Medows to lead the charge against Tipu. When Tipu heard this news, he wrote to Meadows with a proposal to settle differences amicably. However, Medows curtly replied that "an attack upon an ally of the English was tantamount to a declaration of war upon themselves [the British]." This reply alarmed Tipu who had for six years been used to British inaction and hesitation. He left Travancore via Coimbatore and reached Srirangapattana to prepare for the impending war.

Indeed, things were looking really bad for Tipu. Both the number and prowess of his army had dangerously shrunk. At the time of Hyder Ali's death in 1782, the force was a lakh-plus strong. By the end of 1789, it had dwindled by more than fifty per cent. Two significant reasons explain this sorry state. First, there was this large number of soldiers who had died in the various and unncessary wars Tipu had waged during the 1783-89 period; during the same period, a significant number of soldiers had deserted him and joined his enemies' forces. Second, the majority of people in his dominions were Hindus; the number of these Hindus who had volunteered to join the Mysore army during Hyder's time dipped drastically under Tipu's rule.

And then there was also the *Ahmadi* contingent of his army, which comprised the unfortunate Hindus who were captured, forcibly converted, and enlisted into his army during the Malabar and Coorg raids. Tipu awarded thoughtless promotions to these *Ahmadis* simply because they had become Muslims. The direct consequence of this was a loss in his army's competence. When Tipu realized this loss, he requested the French to send a 15000-strong troop. This request was separate from his *other* request for sending Black warriors from Africa whom the French had taken as slaves. However, the French simply ignored this request.

A desperate Tipu now made an appeal to all South Indian Muslim rulers to help him cleanse the land by getting rid of Kaffirs. The appeal was roundly rejected. These were the same Muslim rulers who had been victims of Tipu's wanton attacks in the past. If anything, they were now united *against* him.

Tipu's enemies unite

On 4 July 1790, the treaty between the British, the Nizam and the Marathas against Tipu was ratified. On the side of the British East India Company, it was settled by Captain John

Kennaway and signed by Cornwallis, Charles Stuart, and Peter Speke; on the side of the Marathas, by Peshwa Seway Madhava Rao, and on the side of the Nizam, by Nawab Asaf Jah Bahadur, Subedar of the Deccan. It's interesting to examine some key Articles of the treaty.

Article IX: *....in the event of a peace (with Tipu) being judged expedient, it shall be made by mutual consent...no party...shall... enter into any separate negotiations with Tipu but on the receipt of any advance or message from him by either party, it shall be communicated to the others.*

Article X: *If after the conclusion of peace with Tipu, he should attack or molest either of the contracting parties, the others shall join to punish him, the mode and conditions of effecting which shall be hereafter settled by the contracting powers...*

After the British, the Nizam, and the Marathas had concluded the treaty, the other victims and enemies of Tipu— the various Nawabs, Rajas and Palegars hailing from Arcot, Kadapa, Kurnool, Tanjavur, Travancore, Calicut, the Malabar, Cochin, Cherkala, and Coorg—joined their forces.

On 26 October 1790, the Raja of Coorg entered into a formal treaty with the British against Tipu, which came to be known as the Treaty of Tellichery. The Articles of this treaty bear testimony to the anger and horror that the people of Coorg felt for Tipu. This treaty too is worth examining at some length.

Article II: *Tipu Sultan and his adherents shall be considered as common enemies of both parties...the Kodagu Raja shall admit the English troops at any time to pass through his dominions ...and furnish them with such supplies of provisions as the country can afford at reasonable rates...*

Article IV: *The English East India Company shall engage to do everything in their power to render . the Kodagu Raja* *independent of Tipu, in the same manner as the other powers who have entered into an alliance with the Company...The Raja shall be considered as the friend and ally of the honourable Company...*

Article V: *Should the Raja's family or that of any of his subjects have occasion in the present troubles to take refuge in Tellichery, the Company engages to receive them at the foot of the Ghats and conduct them in safety...a house shall be provided for them during their residence at Tellichery, and the families shall be returned in safety whenever required...*

We don't need any more elaboration as to the kind of cruelties that Tipu had inflicted upon the people of Coorg, and the mortal dread they lived in as a consequence.

The Grand Army of Cornwallis

After securing the friendship of all forces opposed to Tipu, Cornwallis ordered a massive force to march towards Tipu's capital via different routes. He named this force the *Grand Army*, which he led from the front.

From the north, the Grand Army's march began from Dharwad and encamped near Bangalore. Cornwallis led his contingent from Vellore, passed through Kolar and Hosakote before finally arriving in Bangalore on 5 March 1791.

At Bangalore, Cornwallis decided to act immediately, and as a prelude to the Third Anglo-Mysore War, attacked the Bangalore fort the very next day. The attack was led by Colonel Cockrell and Captain Scott of the Bengal Regiment who succeeded in capturing *Pettah* (town) with little resistance from Tipu's army.

Tipu was so enraged at losing *Pettah* that he hanged the Killedar (officer in charge of the fort) in public. Not content, he began to doubt the loyalty of the staff at the Bangalore fort. He punished several of them in public, dismissed everybody and replaced the staff. He then proceeded to mount a strong defence of the fort. A fierce battle ensued for more than two weeks but by 20 March, it was clear to Tipu that all was lost. He abandoned its defence and rushed to Srirangapattana.

While Cornwallis' Grand Army was engaged in action at Bangalore, the Nizam's army had begun marching towards the South.

From the other side, the British Bombay army under General Richard Abercombie had reached Tellichery. There, he mobilized a strong force of Nairs and started ascending the Ghats through Coorg whose Raja provided the assistance (according to the Treaty of Tellicherry) of both troops and logistics. It was this route that the British agent James Sibbald had recommended to the East India Company Government. This massive army, which also included the sizeable force of the Kodagu Raja, marched towards Mysore.

A short while before this force-consolidation occurred, Tipu sent a 5000-strong troop under the leadership of Bahadur Khan to prevent the British from reaching Coorg via the ghats. On 24 February 1791, the Kodagu Raja attacked Bahadur Khan's contingent. The valorous Kodava warriors badly mauled Bahadur Khan's force and killed 400 of his men. Bahadur Khan was effectively hemmed in from all sides and frozen in place without a drop of water. With no avail, he presented himself in person to the Kodagu Raja and called for terms of surrender. The Raja asked him to lay down his arms and surrender. The diary of the English army commander who participated in this war narrates this episode:

Bahadur Khan replied: These are terms to which I cannot accede . were I to accept them, my master would certainly put me to an ignominious death…you, Raja should remember that you are under some obligation to me. You will remember that when you were a prisoner (at Periyapattana) of my master...I not only lightened the burden of your chains, but even at the risk of that life which is now in your possession, both permitted and aided you to escape. Now you have an opportunity to show your love or gratitude and to return the obligation.

The Kodagu Raja showed his gratitude. He let Bahadur Khan and his troops go on the condition that they "must never be seen in and around the region."

Meanwhile, the Maratha army had reached Chitradurga; the Nizam's army had already encamped at Gurramakonda; the Bombay unit of the British army under General Abercombe had reached the borders of Coorg, and the Bengal and Madras regiments of the British army had already captured Bangalore. The stage was set for besieging Srirangapattana from all sides.

The Maratha army was led by senior generals like Haripant, Banna Bapu, and Parashuram Bhau. The British army was led by had war veterans like Captain Little. While Parashuram Bhau began to capture fort after fort starting with Chitradurga, Banna Bapu did likewise in the Shimoga and Bidanur regions. The Nizam's army on its part occupied Tipu's territories in the Gurramakonda region. In other words, Cornwallis' Grand Army had in one fell swoop wrested all of Tipu's prized territories. The manner in which Cornwallis captured Tipu's territories reveals the strategic genius of Cornwallis.

1. The Madras regiment had wrested control (of Tipu's possessions) in Coimbatore, Palghatcheri, Bangalore, Rayakottai, Dindigul, Dharapuram, Hosur, Nandi durga (Nandi Hills), Chitradurga, Pinagra and Sheriyaguri.

2. The Bombay regiment had seized Cannanore, Shimlipattana, Kuttanadu, Chou-ghat, Periyapattana, Irkur, Trenakalur, and Farookhabad.

3. The Maratha army, which was accompanied by Captain Little, had launched a joint operation and captured Dharwad, Bankapur, Holehonnur, and Shimoga.

4. The Nizam whose army had joined hands under the leadership of Major Montgomery and Captain Reed had taken control of Koppal, Ganjikota, Gurramakonda, and Kollegal.

To Tipu, the writing was clear: the ultimate goal of the Grand Army was the capture of Srirangapattana.

So what did Tipu, the Tiger of Mysore do? Did he, like a tiger bare his fangs and give the Grand Army the fight of its life? The answer: he wrote a letter to the British Governor at Madras. A letter, which indicated that this Tiger had folded its tail in surrender and supplication.

14

The Tiger of Mysore Gave up even before the War Began

By February 1792, the British and their allies had captured more than three-fourths of Tipu's dominions. On the forenoon of 5 February 1792, the Grand Army had laid siege to the fort of Srirangapattana. On 7 February 1792, Cornwallis ordered an assault of the fort.

But Tipu's troubles only began to mount. Discontent was brewing in his army. Thanks to his hot-headed stubbornness and staunch refusal to accept reality, several of Tipu's key commanders and generals began to display resentment openly. Kamaruddin, one of Tipu's most trusted generals provides a good illustration of this fact. Kamaruddin was a battle-hardened veteran, experienced and shrewd. More importantly, unlike his master, he didn't allow his commonsense to be clouded by his vanity. When he saw the rapidity with which the Grand Army was making inroads, he warned Tipu that it was best to sue for peace early on. As was his wont, Tipu rejected his recommendation. A hapless Kamaruddin simply deserted his post at Coimbatore. Here is the 1792 *Madras Courier* report describing the event:

*Reports are prevalent in the [Grand Army] camp that Kamaruddin had revolted, or in other words, that he had erected an independent standard. His declared purpose is peace, and **he is joined by great numbers [of supporters] daily**...it is tolerably certain that [Kamaruddin] has resented the conduct of Tipu Sultan* *in the breach of the capitulation of Coimbatore. He has represented it as derogatory to his own honour, and such a violation of all good faith, that no power in future will ever confide in [Tipu's] word....* **and he has declared publicly that if Tipu will not ratify the treaty, he will no longer serve him.** (Emphasis added)

Pretty self-explanatory. It also shows in what regard Tipu's own men held him. Kamaruddin's reference to the capitulation of Coimbatore is explained by Tipu's 24 January 1792 letter to the British Governor at Madras:

Your Lordship's letter arrived...in effecting the affairs of peace between the four powers (Tipu, the Nizam, the Marathas and the British, your Lordship is not neglectful of yourself, but that the garrison of Coimbatore, who surrendered a capitulation, and are in confinement, must be released; that after their arrival, the Vakils [negotiators] of the three Sarkars shall assemble at a certain place, and such negotiations as may be necessary shall then be commenced...

Someone has reported [things] falsely to your Lordship. Sometime ago when the troops of Ahmadi Sarkar [Tipu referred to his Government by that name] besieged Dharapuram, the garrison surrendered one capitulation and were immediately furnished with an escort and tent to your Lordship's army. God forbid! It is not the practice of any state to confine those whose release may have been stipulated by agreements...

A confidential agent shall be sent to you from the Ahmadi Sarkar that the negotiations for peace maybe entered with your Lordship, with the Peshwa or with Nizam Ali Khan, that through your Lordship's means the peace and quiet maybe effected.

A close reading of this letter reveals interesting things. First, the letter does contain an offer for peace—that Tipu was willing to conclude a treaty of peace with the British. However, the tone of the letter doesn't display the attitude of the vanquished towards the victor. Second, Tipu was calling for peace negotiations with the British, the Marathas and the Nizam although the Marathas and the Nizam had no part in the trouble at the Coimbatore fort. Third, by the time he wrote this letter, Cornwallis' Grand Army had wrested more than sixty per cent of his territory and were marching towards his capital. Thus, it was more accurately a frightened coward's desperate plea than anything else.

But by that date, there was no chance that neither the Madras Governor nor Cornwallis would agree to Tipu's peace proposal.

A Painting of the Third Anglo Mysore War

Tipu becomes a prisoner in his own home

The siege of 5 February was so exceptionally effective that in just a day, that is, on 6 February 1792, the Grand Army had completely surrounded the fort of Srirangapattana. It was almost a walkover for the British. But the walkover owed to the careful and meticulous reconnaissance of the entire city and fort, an effort that Cornwallis personally directed. In the words of I.M. Muthanna:

The English engineers had surveyed the entire vicinity of [Srirangapattana] and thereafter the Army had taken positions at vantage points. The English army had broken all barricades and obstacles and then marched ahead nearer [Srirangapattana]. *Tipu's calculations had proved wrong. Earl Cornwallis, Abercrombie, Medows, and Maxwell led their contingents from their posts but the Grand Army alone was enough to finish off the war...[W]ithin a short time, the English acquired* [the French General in Tipu's service] *'Lally's Battery.'*

Tipu was hemmed in and became a prisoner in his own home.

On the evening of 6 February 1792, Cornwallis ordered his troops to open fire on Tipu's fort, and from 7 February onwards, the firing and shelling only intensified. There were of course minor skirmishes between the allied forces and that of Tipu but it was evident that the Tiger of Mysore had abandoned the pretence of putting up even a token resistance. The allied army had quite easily "gathered a good deal of provisions and loot." In fact, the following passage from an on-the-spot report of this war published in the February 1792 edition of *Madras Courier* is an eloquent testimony to the much-touted courage and bravery of the Tiger of Mysore:

...the...two abundant defences [Tipu] has thrown up round his capital, are all characteristic of the man or rather the monster, and highly indicative of those fears and apprehensions [concerning the Grand Army's attack] of his! **Shut up within the walls of Srirangapattana which he dares not quit**, *he ruminates on all the horrors of his situation...and exercises his native cruelty through the means of those who yet adhere to his interests, and are base enough to aid his purpose.*

[...]

The circumstances corroborate the fact that nothing but confusion and despair reign in the Durbar of the once most proud Sultan...Tipu sees his usurped dominions wrested from him, by successive conquests, and that every province of consequence, is in the possession of the confederate [allied] powers. **His troops defeated in every attempt...and finding all their efforts to check or impede our operations vain and ineffectual, they are no longer to be deceived by...[Tipu's] promises but giving way to their situation and in a state of mutiny, that a number of them have fled with their families determined neither to obey the command nor share the fortunes of their masters.**

Thus circumscribed and hopeless, **the once imperious tyrant no longer assumes the haughty tones of the insulting despot, but trembling at his approaching destiny. He bends to the prowess of our arms, and...is anxious only to receive peace on any terms**. (Emphasis added)

If this was not enough, Tipu secretly directed a small group of his trusted men to transport his treasure to Chitradurga. However, as luck would have it, this surreptitious activity was spotted by the British who did not allow Tipu's men to proceed, and forced them back to Srirangapattana. This is *yet* another instance of Tipu's cowardice—he preferred to secure his personal wealth and safety than stand up and defend his fort.

But Tipu's cowardice was only matched by his procrastination, a futile hope that the problem would go away if he kept stalling it. On the one side he kept sending

Allied Forces Attack Tipu's Fort.

feelers of peace but continually rejected the terms proposed by the allied forces.

By now, his fort was badly battered, he had lost thousands of soldiers, and large numbers of his own men either disobeyed his orders or deserted him. And so, on 14 February, Tipu sent word for peace negotiations. On 15 February, his vakils (negotiators) arrived at the venue fixed for the talks. The British sent Sir John Kennaway and the Marathas and the Nizam sent their respective vakils. Tipu did not agree to the terms set by his enemies. Here is the account verbatim, taken from the March 15 1792 report published in the *Calcutta Gazette*.

Tipu's French troops and cavalry continue to desert him in great numbers, and it is said that Lally's son also meditates the same step...

Camp: 16 February 1792: The Vakils have met again, and Tipu is quiet...Our preparations are going on briskly and he will not have much time to deliberate. Gen Abercrombie's army has joined and encamped on our right...Tipu has his family, treasures, shroffs, and merchants all in it [Srirangapattana]...The deserters say that there is great consternation...in the Fort and they are kept quiet only by the assurance of peace.

Meanwhile, the Maratha general, Parashuram Bhau had reached the allied camp at Srirangapattana on 17 February 1792. The other commander of the Maratha army Haripant, was down with fever but the Maratha army was charged up for battle.

When Tipu learned of this, he was in no doubt as to the enormity of what awaited him. Between 14 and 18 February, Tipu kept sending his vakils for peace talks, all of which failed because he simply refused to accept the terms set by the allies. Even more foolishly, he kept firing at the allied posts. On their part, the allies began shelling his fort relentlessly each time peace talks collapsed. To quote I.M. Muthanna,

The peace talks were going on, sometimes with abrupt suspensions, while Tipu continued to fight a losing battle with all his enemies safely sitting in and around the fort of Srirangapattana and dictating peace terms to him...There was no way for the vanquished Tipu Sultan to impose his terms in the peace treaty because the victors, especially the English, the Nizam and the Marathas would not budge from their standpoint, and when there was hesitation on the part of Tipu...the firing and shelling of the fort continued for several days.

When the allies finally realized that Tipu was just stalling them, they intensified their assault. On 20 and 21 February, the Grand Army battered Tipu's fort without a break. On 23 February, Tipu yielded.

Tipu Surrenders

Tipu signs a humiliating treaty

On the night of 23 February 1792 at 9 P.M., a peace treaty was signed by the representatives of the British and their allies, and Tipu. It was a wholly one-sided treaty in which the British gained immensely while Tipu suffered a massive loss of territory, resources, and prestige. He was thoroughly humiliated before the same small chieftains, Rajas, and Nawabs who had once borne the brunt of his barbarities. He was forced to agree to every single condition that was imposed upon him.

He had to cede half of his kingdom, pay three crores and thirty three lakh rupees as war expenses, and the worst of all, had to send two of his sons as hostages "for the due observance of the Treaty in all its parts." Additionally, he promised to release all the prisoners in his custody.

Now, the episode of the British taking two of Tipu's sons as hostages has been given a different colour in present day India mostly by the alleged historians of the Marxist school and an assortment of self-proclaimed secularists. It is used as an illustration that was representative of the innate cruelty of the British. However, facts of history show a different picture. The British had learnt their lessons from the Treaty of Mangalore, which Tipu had violated almost immediately after signing it, and kept violating it with impunity. They had learned that Tipu was not a man to be trusted at any cost. It was to prevent Tipu from repeating his breach of trust that the British took his sons as hostages for two years.

Besides, as Dr S L Bhyrappa mentions, taking children of the defeated enemy as hostages was a practice inaugurated by Muslim rulers in India. One wonders why our Marxists should cry hoarse when the British did the same to Tipu. And on reasonable grounds.

Cornwallis Receives Tipu's Sons.

Tipu appointed Ghulam Ali Khan and Ali Raza as his vakils to see the treaty to its logical end. On 26 February 1792, Tipu sent his second and third son to the custody of the British. Hari Pant and Azmi-ul-Omrah, the respective officers from the Marathas and the Nizam were witnesses to these proceedings.

The allies treated Tipu's sons with great courtesy and respect. When they arrived at the allied camp, they were greeted with a 21-gun salute. Cornwallis embraced them at the entrance of his camp as a mark of welcome and gifted a gold watch to each son.

Thus ended the Third Anglo-Mysore War, which was in reality no war at all. It was a one-sided affair from start to end.

This comprehensive defeat shattered Tipu's arrogance.

Ironically, Tipu had been part of numerous expeditions first under Hyder Ali and then on his own. He had successfully captured several forts after laying siege to them. Some of these forts proved to be a tough challenge. They were difficult to approach, were well-guarded, and the siege often took months to fructify. However, it is surprising that despite having a massive army in his own capital and remaining within the safety of his own strong fort, Tipu managed to capitulate in a mere 20 days and giving up almost without a fight.

Although the British had delivered a decisive blow to Tipu, they proved to be short-sighted in allowing him to remain on the throne of Mysore.

15

The Truth about Tipu's Gifts to Hindu Temples

If Aurangzeb was the most fanatical Muslim king who reigned on the Mughal throne in Delhi at the start of the 18th century, his counterpart who matched him in both bigotry and cruelty in South India at the close of the same century was Tipu Sultan.

Aurangzeb inflicted untold atrocities on Hindus, their way of life, their traditions, and their places of worship over a long period of 50 years. However, when we recall that Tipu inflicted the same—if not greater—kind of barbarism on Hindus within just 17 years, we realize the breadth and depth of his religious zealotry. Aurangzeb had almost all of India as the playground for his fanatical cruelty—Hindus in Delhi, Agra, Rajasthan, Uttar Pradesh, Madhya Pradesh, Gujarat, Kashmir, Punjab, and Haryana bore the extremities of his fanaticism. However, Tipu held sway over large parts of Karnataka, a few regions in Kerala, Tamil Nadu, and Andhra Pradesh. Within this comparatively small area, he managed to foist every kind of brutality imaginable in such a short span of time. His atrocities were not limited to the lives of Hindus—it was all pervasive; it targeted their traditions, places of worship, society, and women.

The British historian Lewis Rice who wrote the *History of Mysore and Coorg* says how in the

...vast empire of Tipu Sultan on the eve of his death, there were only two Hindu temples having daily pujas within the Srirangapattanam fortress. It is only for the satisfaction of the Brahmin astrologers who used to study his horoscope that Tipu Sultan had spared those two temples. The entire wealth of every Hindu temple was confiscated before 1790 itself mainly to make up for the revenue loss due to total prohibition in the country."

Equally, M.H. Gopal in his *Tipu Sultan's Mysore: an Economic History* says that

Mussulmans were exempted from paying the housetax and taxes on grain and other goods meant for their personal use and not for trade. Christians were seized and deported to the capital, and their property confiscated. Converts to Islam were given concessions such as exemption from taxes...[Tipu] removed Hindus from all administrative posts and replaced them with Mussulmans with the exception of Diwan Purnaiah... Another change was the introduction of Persian as the medium of accounts in the revenue department. It was so far the practice in Mysore... to make out the revenue accounts in Kannada, fair copies of which were communicated to the amildars who had them translated into Marathi.

And then we have Tipu's barbaric raid on the Malabar, which we have already seen in some detail. There is no atrocity that he didn't commit on the Hindus there, no measure for the rivers of Hindu blood he shed, no limit to the cruelties he inflicted. It is worth recalling William Logan's list of the Hindu temples that Tipu destroyed in the Malabar. It is also worth recalling the frenzy of rapture Tipu felt after his Malabar raid. He describes this rapture in his 19 January 1790 letter to his loyal servant, Badruz Juman Khan:

I have achieved a great victory recently in Malabar and over four lakh Hindus were converted to Islam. I am now determined to march against the cursed Raman Nair.

Tipu Meets the Sringeri Pontiff.

This Raman Nair was the same Dharmaraja Raman Nair of Travancore. This determination cost Tipu dearly. As we have seen in earlier chapters, it directly led to the so-called Third Anglo Mysore war, which badly singed Tipu. His hubris lay in tatters, and he appeared to have softened at least outwardly.

His immediate objective was to recover half of his kingdom, which he had to surrender to the British, according to the 1792 treaty. He realized that in order to achieve this objective, he could not afford to antagonize the Hindus who formed the majority population in his remaining dominions.

It was in this circumstance that he gave grants and gifts to the Mutt at Sringeri. However, our self-proclaimed intellectuals and alleged historians hold such aberrations as proof of Tipu's amazing religious tolerance. However, if we examine the conditions under which Tipu wrote honey-dipped letters to the pontiff of Sringeri and made lavish donations to the Mutt, a completely different picture emerges. Leela Prasad, in her *Poetics of conduct: oral narrative and moral being in a South Indian town* quotes Surendranath Sen,

Tipu was at this time [in 1793] hard-pressed by his enemies and wanted, therefore, to conciliate his Hindu subjects and at the same time to bring about the discomfiture of his enemies [the Marathas] by means of . superstitious rites.

This reveals another facet of Tipu's personality.

Tipu placed immense faith in astrology. He filled his court with all sorts of soothsayers and astrologers. He would consult them for fixing auspicious dates and times before embarking on a raid. In his book, *Life History of Raja Kesavadas,* V. R. Parameswaran Pillai narrates Tipu's obsession with astrology:

With respect to the much-published land-grants I had explained the reasons about 40 years back. Tipu had immense faith in astrological predictions. It was to become an Emperor (Padushah) after destroying the might of the British that Tipu resorted to land-grants and other donations to Hindu temples in Mysore including Sringeri Mutt, as per the advice of the local Brahmin astrologers. Most of these were done after his defeat in 1791 and the humiliating Srirangapatanam Treaty in 1792. These grants were not done out of respect or love for Hindus or Hindu religion but for becoming Padushah as predicted by the astrologers.

The British Colonel and historian, William Kirkpatrick who discovered more than 2000 letters (written in Farsi in Tipu's own handwriting) in Tipu's Srirangapattana fort (after Tipu's death) also echoes Parameswaran Pillai:

in his childish eagerness to give new denominations to everything, he should have suffered Seringapatam [Srirangapattana] and Bangalore to retain their old names; especially as the former appellation, having been derived from an idol, might, on that account, be supposed to have been particularly offensive to a bigoted Musulman. It is not, therefore, improbable, that some superstitious notion may have restrained him in these instances.

Tipu's confidence had been shattered by a series of reverses, which had finally culminated in the humiliating defeat of 1792. In this war, he had to cough up a huge sum of money, surrender half his territory, and had to send two of his sons as hostages. The haughty Tipu of the 1782-92 decade now faced an uphill struggle to recover his territory and regain his wounded pride. He had finally realized that in order to face a tough enemy like the British, he had to earn the confidence of his Hindu subjects who formed the majority population. He also understood that he would be in great personal danger if he antagonized them any further.

Therefore, it is more accurate to say that Tipu's donation to the Sringeri Mutt was born out political expediency and not religious tolerance. If he was indeed a tolerant ruler, why would he demolish so many Hindu temples throughout his kingdom and in that of others? Why would he engage in such rampant and large scale conversions of Hindus? Why would he, in his secret letters, address non-Muslims as Kaffirs?

It was the politician in Tipu that gave donations, grants, and gifts to the Sringeri Mutt and a few other temples. The bigot in him remained intact, eclipsed temporarily by a humiliating setback.

16

A Treacherous Pact with the French

Meanwhile, the British misgivings about Tipu began to slowly unravel.

The British took two sons of Tipu as hostages as part of the treaty of the Third Anglo-Mysore for a reason: they did not trust him. After about two years, they were proved right. Although Tipu didn't attach any value to things like keeping one's word, the British on their part, behaved honourably. They released Tipu's sons after he paid three crore rupees as war indemnity.

However, Tipu showed his charlatanism yet again.

Contemporary history books inform us that Tipu joined hands with the French in order to drive the British out of India. This spurious fact is upheld as proof of his patriotism. However, what was Tipu's real intent behind allying himself with the French?

In reality, Tipu saw no difference between the British and the French. His religious fanaticism had clouded any sense of balance. In his eyes, the French, the British, the Portuguese, the Dutch...everybody were enemies of Islam. His own letters confirm this fact.

As we have seen, it was Hyder Ali who first built cordial relations with the French. The political conditions prevailing at that time caused the cementing of this relationship. It so happened that anybody Hyder Ali fought against turned out to be friends with the British and therefore, opponents of the French. Thus, there was no chance that the British even considered the option of shaking hands with Hyder Ali. The politics of Europe also contributed to this in some measure. In Europe, the British and French were engaged in continuous hostilities against each other in the 18th century. This conflict was in many ways, extended to and in India. In this battle with the British, the French had no one to ally with in the whole of South India except Hyder Ali. In a way, the French and Hyder Ali became inevitable to each other.

Tipu consumed with revenge

During the two or three years after the Third Anglo-Mysore war, Tipu brooded over his defeat and finally decided that his only option was to escalate his friendship with the French. Revenge was on his mind. He forgot the fact that wooing the French would be contrary to the terms of the 1792 treaty. He sent his old French friend, the envoy Pierre Monneron to see the former Governor of Pondicherry, D.C. Cossigny and his brother Jacques who were residing in Mauritius (then a French colony). The mission appeared to be a success. Monneron met Cossigny and returned to Srirangapattana with a letter from him containing mellifluous "tributes to Tipu's greatness." Cossigny also assured Tipu of French support and service.

Tipu had come to a decisive conclusion in the wake of his mortifying defeat in 1792. Because he had no friend in all of India, he concluded that it was best to befriend a foreigner to oust another foreigner. Pierre Monneron's assurance of support came as a huge relief for Tipu. It set in motion a long and cozy friendship between Tipu and the French, which lasted till his death. He drafted a Treaty of Alliance with the French, which Monneron took with him when he left for Paris in 1796 with Rear Admiral Sercey. The main provisions of the Tipu—Monneron document are as follows:

1. The French are to send 10,000 troops to attack Tellicherry. After burning it, they are to join forces with the Mysoreans with Tipu in supreme command and march towards Cochin, Madura, Trichinopoly [Tiruchinapalli] and Tanjore.

2. With these [regions] placed firmly in their hands, there is to be a joint advance on Pondicherry and Madras, and thence by land to capture Calcutta. From there follows a sweep across the sub-continent to Bombay which, said Tipu, the French may have for their own.

3. Tipu on his side promises to provide 5000 troops to every 1000 French troops. But he stipulated that his name must appear as their ally in any future peace treaty between France and England, and because he has been "unable to take any revenge upon the English," such a treaty must stipulate that Great Britain must return his territory and pay him 300 lakh rupees back."

The Cossigny brothers fully agreed with these points. Their reasoning was based on the English-French conflict in Europe. They concluded that because the British would be busy in Europe, they wouldn't be able to afford to send more troops to India. Additionally, the British had a force of about 12,000 Europeans and 40,000 sepoys, busy attacking Dutch possessions in the Indian Ocean in 1795. Tipu on his part reasoned that he had a massive and well-trained force which would be supplemented by French troops. The plan therefore, was to take this huge force and conquer all of India. However, the Cossigny brothers also expressed some reservations about granting full control of the operations to Tipu as well as the amount of war spoils he should get.

Tipu and the French began serious correspondence in the beginning of 1797. Tipu was in touch not just with the Cossigny brothers but with M. Raymond who headed the French army in Hyderabad. Tipu also used the service of Francois Ripaud who was employed in his court at Srirangapattana. Ripaud became the go-between for the French in Mauritius and Tipu. In one of the letters, Tipu reminds the French of their relationship, which dated back to Hyder Ali's days. In yet another, he chides the

...ambitious English, not having sufficient confidence in their own strength and courage to attack me singly, formed an alliance with the Marathas and the Nizam...and attacked me in every quarter. At the very moment when I was on the point of conquering them, the French army under the command of Monsieur de Cossigny, received an order from Mon. de Bussy to abandon me...but what filled me with indignation was that these orders extended to Mon. de Lally who commanded a body of French in my pay, to withdraw himself from the party...Reduced single to my own resources and abandoned by my allies, I was compelled to make peace with the loss of half of my dominions and money in Rupees 3.30 crores.

It is clear from this letter that he felt bad that the French had let him down in this war, and requested in the same letter not to abandon him once again.

Tipu wrote these letters in Farsi. After his fall, the British meticulously organized, catalogued, and filed these letters. Every letter was named and numbered under the head, "French Correspondence." The letters were translated into English by G.G. Keble, and provide a whole new outlook to the nature of Tipu's politics.

Tipu also took care not to reveal his religious bigotry in any of his renewed correspondence with the French. Although he wasn't a political or military strategist of any reckoning, the fact he was able to conceive such a plot was surprising. On their part, the French kept up the appearance of giving him highly positive feedback for every single scheme however outrageous or impossible it appeared. They saw no point in antagonizing him; on the contrary, they discovered that flattering him resulted in enormous pecuniary benefit for them. And so, until the very end, the French kept seducing Tipu with promises and assurances but did nothing on the ground.

Tipu misleads the French

But then Tipu was on a grievous mission to seek revenge. His hand of friendship towards the French quickly became desperate pleas. This desperation even led him to paint a faulty picture of the actual situation in India to the French. Tipu's Letter Number 15 (as arranged by the translators, Keble and Edmondstone) makes for revealing reading:

According to the news from Hyderabad, Nizam Ali Khan is extremely ill...He has three or four sons inimical to one another. Several of them solicit the protection of Our Sarkar [Tipu]...

As to the Marathas, the head of the State threw himself off the top of the house and was killed. All the chiefs are inimical to one another...they no longer possess any authority throughout the country. The troops of Zaman Shah [the Afghan ruler] have reached Delhi, the capital of the Mughal emperor. He himself had come with him. The Maratha troops have appeared in and around Delhi. All the chiefs of Hindustan are disaffected to the Marathas on account of their oppression. There is no doubt that they will soon be expelled from there.

The domestic disputes of the two Sardars [the Nizam and the Marathas] will certainly prevent either of them from joining the English. At the desire and instigation of Zaman Shah...the late vizier of Assaf Daulah has quarreled with the English, assembled his army and is prepared for hostilities against them. The English likewise have assembled their army in Bengal. In Calicut, the Raja Kotanchery has slain in battle "a thousand Englishmen" and many more native chiefs and soldiers. The whole of Calicut district is rendered disaffected by the oppression and violence of the English. In various places the inhabitants are in arms and they do not acknowledge the English authority. The Palegars of Masulipatna, Vellore and Arcot districts are also ready to revolt. In short, now is the moment of opportunity.

The following, a 2 April 1797 letter to General Malartic stationed on the Isle of France, is yet another sample:

Delhi is thrown into confusion by the arrival of king Zaman Shah, my friend, who has attacked the Marathas and completely defeated them. The Marathas rallied on the English who could not assist him...

It is unclear why Tipu wrote such patently misleading letters to the French who had their own intelligence network, which was vastly superior to that of Tipu. It is said that Tipu's spies conveyed such false accounts to him in a bid to earn the good offices of their Sultan, and the Sultan in turn believed them to be true and relayed them to the French after adding his own dose of exaggerations. However, when we examine the entire corpus of Tipu's letters to the French, it is clear that he intentionally provided a deceptive picture of the situation under the illusion that he was implementing a grand political strategy. However, Tipu had failed to realize an important reality.

The France of that era was ruled by Napoleon Bonaparte who singlehandedly had made it arguably the most powerful nation in Europe. The French army apart from being numerically large was also one of the best in the world. And France's competent intelligence network could easily call Tipu's bluff on matters related to the Indian situation. It is therefore stunning when we notice how Tipu overlooked this simple reality and continued to feed apparent falsehoods to the French.

In a letter dated 21 April 1797, he wrote:

The Nizam, an ally of the English, and the chief of the Mughals, is very ill, and his age leaves no precept of his recovery. He has four children who are disputing the right of succession. One of them is much attached to me, is the favourite of the people, and is expected to succeed him...

Even as he wrote this letter, Tipu had put a plot in motion in the Nizam's dominions. He managed to establish contact with one of the Nizam's sons and instigated him to rebel against his father. It is unclear whether the Nizam knew that Tipu was the puppeteer behind this rebellion. However, he nipped it in the bud and threw his son into jail. Ironically, it was the French in the Nizam's army who played a major role in suppressing this rebellion!

The postscript of that 21 April 1797 letter is even more interesting:

Since writing this letter, I have learnt by an Arab ship that great disturbance has prevailed in Bengal. The arrival of the Nawab Zaman Shah at Lucknow has made the English tremble, and particularly at Calcutta they are in great consternation as they are unable to prevent Mir Asaf-ud-Daulah from joining Zaman Shah. It appears that both these princes are determined to be revenged of the English. Send me the troops to join with mine, so that I too may treat them as they deserve.

The tone and tenor of this letter clearly indicates that Tipu wanted to convey to the French the impression that he was good friends with the local Muslim rulers who had joined hands with a foreign Muslim invader against the British. Therefore, if the French would send their forces to his aid, the combined army would be formidable, and the British would be easily driven out of India. What he did not disclose to the French was the fact that he was already in correspondence with various Sultans in Asia, seeking their support on the plank of establishing the kingdom of Islam in India.

However, the French showed no interest in Tipu's grand scheme. Like Hyder Ali, Tipu had forgotten the Treaty of Versailles where the French had retired from the race of rivalry with the British in India. Besides, the French influence and dominions in India had woefully shrunk, and their correspondence and assurances to Tipu were merely eyewash. Tipu never realized this fact till the end, and kept courting them in vain. He actually believed that the French would send a large army to his aid, and drafted lengthy treaties to the effect. In one such treaty, he mentioned that

French soldiers about 10,000, Negroes [Habshis] about 30,000 to be landed [in India]; ships of war suitable to the number of troops to be in attendance at sea until the conclusion of the war...the army shall land in Mirjan...and affording effectual aid, shall bring the fort of Goa into the possession of this Sarkar [Tipu's government].

Tipu also sought the opinion of his key ministers and army officers on the subject of befriending the French. Muhammad Reza, the "Mir Mirjan" or commander of Tipu's army gave his opinion in a letter he jointly signed with Diwan Purnayya:

In spite of the expenditure of so large a sum of money, the insincerity, faithlessness and refractory disposition of the French are evident...without their making over to this Sarkar the district of Calicut, it does not appear advisable to us that they should be permitted to land in any of your Highness's ports and be furnished with provisions.

However, Tipu ignored such warnings and continued pursuing his dream project of a grand Franco-Mysore Alliance. He sent a delegation to Mauritius with specific instructions. If the French outpost there failed to respond favourably to Tipu's proposal, the delegation was to travel to France and open negotiations directly with the French Government. Hasan Ali and Muhammad Ibrahim set out for Mauritius along with Ripaud. They left from Mangalore on 5 December 1797 and reached Mauritius on 19 January 1798. This trip was supposed to be secret.

Upon landing in Mauritius, the French accorded the treatment befitting a state guest to these two envoys. Tipu had requested (in two letters) from the French a force comprising 30,000 cavalry, 40,000 infantry, and 100 guns. The French received the request and promised to forward it to the Government in France. On 23 January 1798, these two letters were dispatched to France on board a warship.

The British intensified their watch on Tipu

Meanwhile, the British and their allies were keenly watching these alarming developments even as Tipu heedlessly courted the French and opened up communication with various Muslim kings in West Asia. Spies of the British and their allies reported every move of Tipu. A plan for a final and decisive assault against Tipu began to slowly materialize.

The French too, got wind of this development but continued to mislead Tipu. They promised armed and other forms of assistance on the condition that Tipu pay them a premium this time. They demanded a year's salary as advance payment. In July and August 1798, the French General D. Buc wrote a series of letters to Tipu warning him of the British design on Srirangapattana. In one letter, he stated that he had information that "Lord Mornington, Governor-General of Bengal, and General Clarke are expected on the coast [of Madras] at the end of this month for the purpose of entering upon a negotiation with your Majesty, which [if not] successful, will be followed by a declaration of war." He urged Tipu that "[y]our time is short and precious," and that he must prepare for war immediately.

The British had realized that Tipu had proven to be untrustworthy again. He had violated the Treaty of 1792 by courting the French, and by inviting the Muslim kings of Iran, Turkey, and Afghanistan to wage Jihad in India. The British intent of pressing for a fresh treaty with Tipu under the leadership of Lord Mornington was to prevent him from carrying out his designs. In the event the treaty failed, the British plan was to mount a final attack against him like before, with the support of all their allies.

General De Buc of course, knew of this British plan. In his letter dated 16 December 1798—perhaps the last correspondence the French had with Tipu—De Buc urged Tipu to "convince the English of your good intentions. Anticipate the English by your activity and throw impediments in their way..." Tipu by now had realized the danger that was confronting him. In his reply to De Buc, he wrote that it was now dangerous to even exchange correspondence in this manner because letters were being intercepted by enemy agents, and added that "if you should write again, mention no names." He made a last, desperate attempt to make peace with the Marathas by sending his envoys to Poona but failed. Equally, he rejected the second offer of peace from the British side. Till the very end, Tipu laboured under an illusory confidence of securing massive aid from the French and Muslim kings abroad.

It needs to be recalled that Tipu's exertions to drive the British out of India did not originate from patriotic intentions. It originated in his grandiose dream of establishing an Islamic Empire in India. It was to achieve this goal that Tipu made an agreement to divide India equally between himself and the French. He dictated the draft of this agreement to his Munshis (clerks/copyists). The agreement (in Farsi, and comprising 14 Articles) reproduced in its entirety is an eloquent, first hand testimony to Tipu's "patriotism" and punctures claims of his being a "national hero."

i) *The French Sarkar or the French troops should never do anything without consulting us nor agree to conclude peace without our approval.*

ii) *The French generals and troops shall undertake nothing without first consulting us concerning the common interests in respect of war.*

iii) *If any French officers or men should excite disturbances or treachery in the Army of our Sarkar, the circumstances should be reported to us. The offenders should be punished according to their [French] customs.*

iv) *After the war, the amount of the expense should be settled between the French and this Sarkar in fair terms.*

v) *All conquests and capture of territory, effects, forts, money, articles, grain, ships, sea-coasts, etc to be equally divided among us and the French.*

vi) *Whatever territory belonging to the English, be taken under this alliance with the French in conjunction with the troops of our Sarkar, shall be divided.*

vii) *On the reduction of the fort of Goa, it shall be retained by our Sarkar, and in like manner, the Bombay fort shall be assigned to the French.*

viii) *All English and Portuguese prisoners, male and female, shall be allowed subsistence allowance, and be kept in confinement till the war ends.*

ix) *About the forts, territories, etc that are to be divided, it shall depend upon our mutual decision as to what forts are to be garrisoned and which others are to be destroyed.*

x) *As an easiest means of effecting the expulsions of the English and the Portuguese, let us be supplied by the*

	French with five to ten thousand Europeans and about 30,000 Negroes—all trained men.
xi)	*The French troops shall disembark at Honnawar and then proceed to Goa. The advantage of taking Goa is that there will be a place for the ships to remain and the troops could easily be supplied with necessary equipment.*
xii)	*After having fully considered these propositions, let us have speedy intelligence…An European contingent will be stationed on the sea-coast.*
xiii)	*Four persons in our confidence are being deputed, and, of these, we request that you will despatch two, upon one of your ships to France…to carry on negotiations there…You will also get our ship coppered.*
xiv)	*While engaged in attacking the English and the Portuguese, should the Marathas and the Nizam assist them, we must chastise them effectively.*

On 2 April 1797, Tipu wrote another draft agreement comprising five Articles. This agreement was similar to the aforementioned one except for Article IV, which states that

The whole of the British territorial possessions in Hindustan shall be reduced. Half of the country and the forts and stores, shall be taken over by our Sarkar and the other half made over to the French…the country and the forts of our Sarkar which the English wrested in 1792 are not to be included in the partition between the French and our Sarkar…the fort of Goa shall be possessed by our Sarkar and that of Bombay shall be made over to the French.

Equally, this also shows the extent of Tipu's delusions of conquering the entire country with French help! Besides, another interesting insight emerges from such daydreams of Tipu.

Tipu repeatedly requested French help with absolutely no knowledge of the political situation in Europe at the time. It is a different matter that the French didn't give him assistance till the end. However, Tipu's unrealistic reveries had attracted the attention of Napoleon Bonaparte who actually wrote a few letters to Tipu. One of these letters, recovered on 17 February 1799 (after Tipu's death), makes for interesting reading:

Headquarters at Cairo, 7th Year of the Republic; One and Indivisible! From Bounaparte, Member of the National Convention, General in Chief, to the Most Magnificent Sultan, Our Great Friend, Tipu Saheb. You have already been informed of my arrival on the borders of the Red Sea, with an innumerable and invincible army full of desire of delivering you from the iron yoke of England. I eagerly embrace this opportunity of testifying to you the desire I have of being informed by you, by the way of Muscat and Mocha. As to your political situation, I would wish you could send some intelligent person to Suez or Cairo, possessing your confidence, with whom I may confer.

This letter was delivered to the Sheriff of Mecca with a note where Napoleon told the Sheriff, "...I now send you a letter for our friend Tipu Sultan: oblige me by forwarding it to his country." Copies of this letter were intercepted and given to a Munshi of the British Captain Wilson by Sheik Suleiman and Muhammad Amin, the Sheriffs. The Persian letters were all translated by N.B. Edmondstone and from French to English by Captain Wilson. Wilson then forwarded them to the Governor at Bombay who in turn forwarded them to the British Governor General at Calcutta.

The British could hardly remain indifferent when they noticed that Bonaparte had himself written to Tipu addressing him as a friend. As a first step to salvage the situation, the British sent peace proposal after peace proposal. Tipu simply ignored every single proposal.

The British now readied themselves for a full and final assault against Tipu.

17

Tipu Invites Foreign Sultans to Wage Jihad against India

Even as Tipu was busy building a solid alliance with the French, he didn't lose sight of the fact that he had to also garner the support of Muslim chiefs of India and West Asia. He used every trick in the book—flattery, sentimentality, and an appeal to unite under the banner of Islam—to persuade them to invade India.

In his dealings with the French, he was careful to omit references to Islam. However, when he wrote to the Caliph, to Zaman Shah of Afghanistan, and to other foreign Muslim rulers, his letters were full of abusive references towards "Kaffirs, the worshippers of many Gods, the followers of false religions," and contained plans for waging a "holy war against the infidels and free the regions of Hindustan."

The Persian drafts of these and other letters were preserved at the records department of Fort William, Calcutta. They were translated by N.B. Edmondstone and made available for publication in the various Gazettes that the East India Company published from time to time.

However, the pseudo-historians of today who glorify Tipu as a great humanist and freedom fighter don't seem to have the inclination or the patience to read these letters. These letters are the first hand evidence that unambiguously show how Tipu was a dangerous Islamic bigot.

Overtures to Zaman Shah

Tipu began courting Muslim rulers as early as 1793. However, he intensified his efforts in 1796 when he began to earnestly court the Afghan ruler, Zaman Shah. The correspondence he exchanged with Zaman Shah contained the outlines—and in some cases, details—of his fantastic but horrifying schemes. By that time, the Mughal power had all but been decimated. Delhi, the seat of Mughal power was firmly in the grip of the Marathas. Indeed, Tipu himself had contemptuously referred to the Mughal ruler as a "useless servant who was in the employ of the Maratha Scindia for a monthly wage of fifteen thousand rupees" openly in his court at Srirangapattana. In other words, Tipu saw the irredeemably weakened Mughal power as an opportunity he could exploit. This was in a way supplemented by Zaman Shah who embarked on a series of raids on North India since 1793.

One part of Tipu's traitorous plan included this: he would use Islam as a tool to provoke the rulers of Iran, Turkey, and Afghanistan to invade India. With their support, Tipu would take over North India. Simultaneously, his friendship with the French would ensure that they would support his attacks on the British in the South. Thus, he would be successful in capturing all of India. On the face of it, this plan appeared realistic. However, in reality, it remained the daydream of a despot comfortably ensconced within the Srirangapattana fort because Tipu didn't allow even the possibility to enter his mind that the British were watching his every move with hawk-eyes. He had apparently learned no lesson from the horrific defeat of 1792. The events that led to the Third Anglo-Mysore war were characterized precisely by Tipu's belief in his own powers as a master strategist while being oblivious to the fact that his enemies too were endowed with strategic thinking.

Tipu approached Zaman Shah first in early 1796. He sent Mir Habibullah and Muhammad Reza as ambassadors to Kabul via Karachi to meet the Governor there. He was careful not to send an overtly political message. His ambassadors were sent on the pretext of a commercial mission that was mainly interested in purchasing horses. Tipu's envoys travelled through Kutch and Karachi by ship and then by land through Baluchistan before finally reaching Kabul. In his letter to Zaman Shah, Tipu stressed on the business aspect of his mission and expressed keen interest in setting up a factory at Karachi. After he gained Zaman Shah's confidence, his ambassadors would slowly unravel Tipu's intent of driving the infidels out of India and establishing the rule of Islam in the country with the Afghan king's assistance.

Tipu exchanged correspondence with Zaman Shah on five or six occasions. On every occasion, he shared his dream of Islamizing India. He abused the Hindus, the British, the French, the Dutch, and the Portuguese as infidels. Tipu also mentioned the "treachery" of the Nizam and his neighbouring Muslim Nawabs who had joined hands with the British against him. The highlights of this correspondence, which are given below, are very revealing:

1. *The imbecility and ruinous condition of the kingdom of Delhi are more obvious than the sun. Delhi, which is one of the seats of the Government of the Muslim faith, has been reduced to this state of ruin so that the infidels altogether prevail; it has become proper and incumbent upon the leaders of the Faithful that uniting together they exterminate the infidels.*

2. *I am very desirous of engaging in this pursuit, but there are three sects of infidels in the way of it, and although when we are united there is little ground for apprehension,*

yet the union of the followers of the Faith is necessary. If that Ornament of the Throne, that conqueror of kingdoms, should adopt (one of the) two plans for effecting this, it will tend to the glory of the Faith. One of the plans is as under.

3. *That your Majesty should remain in your capital and send one of your Number; a man in whom you have confidence, to Delhi with an army; that, this person on his arrival there should make the necessary arrangements, and after deposing the infirm king who has reduced the Faith to this state of weakness, select from among the family someone properly qualified for the Government; he should remain one year for the purpose of settling the country and taking with him the chiefs of the country who are the Rajputs and ... direct his standard towards the Deccan, so that the Brahmins and others may come forward and present themselves to him, whilst I, from this quarter, with the aid of God, will raise the standard of the Holy Wars and make the infidels bow under the sword of Faith. After these shall have been sacrificed to the sword, and no longer exist, the remaining infidels will be nothing. Afterwards, the settlements of the Deccan may be concluded in any manner which shall be mutually agreed upon.*

This was the first of the two plans that Tipu mentioned in his letter. The second was even more disastrous had it been carried out.

If none of your Majesty's noblemen should be sufficiently in your confidence or equal to the undertaking, and if your Majesty should be entirely at ease with respect to the state of your country... it is proposed that you should in person proceed to Delhi, and having made the necessary arrangements there, establish one of your confidential servants in the office of the Vizier and return to your own capital. The person who may be selected...[as the] Vizier must be a man of enterprise and status, that remaining twelve months with his army in Delhi, he may be able to bring under subjection the chiefs of the neighbouring country. The second year, your Majesty should also send from your capital a small army as a reinforcement so that the Vizier...may proceed with the chiefs of Hindustan towards the Deccan. Should those infidel Brahmins direct their power to that quarter, by the grace of God, the hands of the heroes of the Faith in this part of the world shall be raised for their chastisement. After their extirpation, it will be proper to enjoin the Vizier...to fix upon a place of rendezvous and there to meet me and then a proper means may be adopted for the settlement of the country.

Tipu had also sent expensive gifts to Zaman Shah along with these letters. The half a dozen letters that he exchanged more or less followed this pattern. They were the words of a bigoted Muslim who found a compelling necessity for waging a holy war against the inhabitants of a country dominated by Hindus. His 5 February 1797 letter to Zaman Shah is more fervent, severer in tone and morbid in its violence against Hindus:

I have the satisfaction to hear that your Majesty, the Ornament on the throne, the promoter of Faith, the destroyer of the heretics, etc, employs your whole time and exerts every faculty in the support of the enlightened Religion, and is wholly devoted to its cause... In return to this [Zaman Shah's religious piety] nearly a hundred thousand followers of the Faith, nay more, assemble every Friday at the mosques of the capital [Srirangapattana], called the Allah and Aksha mosques, and after the prescribed forms of prayer...as "Grant thy aid, O God, to those who aid the religion of Muhammad....and destroy those who destroy the religion of Muhammad...and pray that the Almighty will render your Majesty who is the supporter of the Faith."

Your Majesty must doubtless have been informed that my exalted ambition is to wage a Holy War...In the midst of this land of heretics, the Almighty protects this tract of Muhammadan dominion like the Ark of Noah and cuts short the extended arm of the abandoned heretic.

Tipu's persistent courting paid off. Zaman Shah finally wrote him a letter, an acceptance of friendship.

Your letter replete with sentiments of friendship and regard, expressing your solicitude for the propagation of the Faith and the extirpation of the abandoned irreligious infidels...for the increase of our dominion and the success of our triumphant banners.

As the object of your well-directed mind is the destruction of the infidels and the extension of the Faith of the Prophet, please God, we shall soon march with our conquering army to wage war with the infidels and try to free those regions from the contamination of those shameless tribes with the edge of [our] swords...

A delightful Tipu wasted no time in replying to his new friend. On 30 January 1799, he wrote that he was aware of the British plan to attack him:

Your Majesty's gracious letter...has given increased [value] to our friendship...You were pleased to write that it was the object of yours to crush the infidels and to propagate the religion of Muhammad; please God, your Majesty would soon proceed with the conquering army to prosecute a holy war against the infidels and heretics...It is my hope...that the oppression of the infidels and polytheists may be destroyed by the avenging sword of those who have been selected by God to exercise dominion...

The English having received intimation of the arrival of the ambassadors of the Sarkar [Tipu's ambassadors] at your Highness's court...have taken umbrage, and in concert with the infidels, taken up arms against me and they have written that they entertain the design to subvert Islam. Many are the words that proceed from their lips but their words are nought but lies.

Tipu had grievously misunderstood the import of a letter that the British Governor General had written to him. The letter dated 3 November 1798 warned Tipu of the dire consequences that would visit him if he continued his dalliances with the French. However, Tipu by now was intoxicated with religious fanaticism thanks to the assurance of Zaman Shah. He mistook the British warning as merely an indication that they knew about his correspondence with the Afghan king and nothing more. He disregarded the warning of his confidant and minister Mir Sadiq who urged him to make peace with the British.

The British had had enough. With his fatuous haughtiness, Tipu had opened himself up for a final attack way before Zaman Shah could send his army to cleanse India of Kafirs and establish the sword of Islam in the country.

18
Tipu Meets his Maker

Zaman Shah wasn't the only Muslim king Tipu courted. He had opened up lines of communication with the king of Persia, Fateh Ali Khan, and the Grand Caliph of Constantinople, Sultan Salim. He had been sending secret letters to the Caliph from as early as 1783.

Tipu's overture to the Caliph backfires

In his letters to the Caliph, he painted a deliberate picture of the British as cruel villains. To do this, he gave a twisted version of events, both contemporary and past. In his letters, the British were the destroyers of Islam and Muslims. They were depicted as heartless mercenaries who attacked his father Hyder Ali, and that it was now his turn to face their wanton aggression.

More importantly, Tipu's letters to the Caliph are eloquent testimonies to his absolute ignorance of global affairs. For starters, Tipu was ignorant of a simple fact: that the Caliph was thick friends with the British, and the sworn enemy of the French!

Now, the French had earned the wrath of the Caliph when they invaded Egypt in 1798. Around the same time, the British had allied with the Muslims in Central Asia and fought against the French. Thus, every letter that Tipu wrote to the Caliph inevitably fell into the hands of the British. This was also why Tipu's projection of himself as a pious Muslim Sultan of India suffering at the hands of the Islam-hating British failed to yield any result from that quarter. Equally, the British informed the Caliph that Tipu was thick friends with the French. While Tipu wrote lengthy and repeated letters to the Caliph warning him against the infidel British and their equally infidel friends, the Caliph wrote back cautioning Tipu that it was actually the French who posed the greatest danger to Islam worldwide! This letter dated 20 September 1798 was the last of a series of letters that the Caliph wrote to Tipu. It was published in full in the Madras Gazette on 14 September 1799 after being translated by J.A. Grant, the Sub-Secretary at Fort William. The following is an excerpt of the Caliph's letter to Tipu:

Disposed towards [the French] in a friendly way and reposing confidence in their friendship which they appeared to profess for us, we gave no ear to many positions and advantageous offers which had been made to us to side with the belligerent powers, but pursuant to our maxims of moderation...we abstained from breaking with [the French]...and firmly observed the line of neutrality...

When no cause existed to interrupt the continuance of peace between two nations, [the French] all of a sudden, have exhibited the unprovoked and treacherous proceedings of which the following is a sketch.

They began to prepare a fleet in one of their harbours... and...embarked a large body of troops and they put also on board several people, versed in the Arabic language, and who had been to Egypt before. They gave the command of that armament to one General Bonaparte who first went to the island of Malta, of which he took possession and thence proceeded direct to Alexandria...and suddenly landed his troops and forcibly entered the town...

Later they published manifestoes in Arabic...stating that their enterprise was not to declare war against the Ottoman port but to attack the shores of Egypt for insults...they had committed against the French merchants in the past—that Peace with the Ottoman Empire was permanent, that those Arabs who should join would be treated well...Later they took possession of Rosetta....It is a standing law amongst nations not to encroach upon each other's territories...a conduct [by the French] so audacious, so unprovoked, so deceitfully sudden on their part, is an undeniable trait of the most extreme insult and treachery.

The Caliph vowed never to forgive the French. In the same letter, he also said that

Egypt is considered as a region of general veneration, from the immediate proximity of the noble city of Mecca...and the sacred town of Medina...

It has been discovered from several letters which have been intercepted that the further project of the French is to divide Arabia...to attack the whole Muhammadan sect...and extirpate all Muslims from the face of the earth.

It is for these cogent motives...that we have determined to repel this enemy...It being certain that in addition to the general ties of religion, the bonds of unity...have been ever firm and permanent with your Majesty [Tipu]...we understand that in consequence of certain secret intrigues carried on by the French in India in order to destroy the settlements and sow dissensions in the provinces of the English [in India], a strict connection is expected to take effect between the French and your Majesty, for whose service they are to send over a corps of troops by the way of Egypt.

We are persuaded that the tendency of the French plans cannot in the present days escape your Majesty's...notice, and that no regard will be given to their deceitful insinuations on your side, and whereas the court of Great Britain is actually at war with them and our Sublime Porte engaged...in repelling their aggression. Consequently, the French are the enemies.

Towards the end of the letter, the Caliph was even more direct. He "sincerely hoped" that Tipu would not

refuse every needful exertion towards assisting your brethren Muslims...towards defending Hindustan itself against the effect of French machinations...We hear that an intimate connection has taken place between you and the French. We hope that...your Majesty will beware of this, and in the event of your having harboured any idea of joining with them, or of moving against Great Britain, you will lay such resolutions aside! We make it our special request that your Majesty will please refrain from entering into any measure against the English. (Emphasis added)

The underlying message of the Caliph's letter was not lost on Tipu. It was now clear to him that as long as he was friends with the French, he would get no support from any Muslim ruler anywhere on the earth. The Caliph was the Supreme Leader of all Muslims in the world, and his letter was also a veiled warning to Tipu to desist from troubling the British by allying with the French. And so, the last ray of Tipu's hope was extinguished just like that.

But as we've seen, Tipu was made of sterner foolishness. He let his impetuosity prevail yet again. He just wouldn't let go of his bid to enlist the Caliph's support. After that chastisement, he began to sing the Caliph's tune: he now referred to the *French* as "traitors" and "kaffirs" in his letters to the Caliph. Needless, the Caliph didn't respond to Tipu after that fateful letter of September 1798.

The British decide to launch a terminal assault on Tipu

Lord Mornington had now taken over as the Governor General. He landed in Madras in May 1798 just when Tipu's emissaries returned to India after their expedition to Mauritius. Over the course of the next month, he received intelligence about Tipu's various missions and correspondences—with the French, Zaman Shah, and the Caliph. In fact, the British intelligence gathering was perhaps the best among all the major powers then in India. The *Madras Government Papers* of the period—more precisely, 1797—1798—are instructive. They contain (almost) daily bulletins flashed to the British Government by its spies in Srirangapattana. It didn't take very long for Mornington to conclude that Tipu hadn't changed one bit despite the serious reverses he suffered in 1792.

He wrote his conclusions in a Minute dated 12 August 1792.

*Since the conclusion of the treaty of [Srirangapattana], the British Government in India have uniformly conducted themselves towards Tipu Sultan not only with the most exact attention to the principles of moderation, justice, and good faith, but have endeavoured by every practicable means to conciliate his confidence, and to mitigate his vindictive spirit...**The act of Tipu's ambassadors, ratified by himself, and accompanied by the landing of a French force in his country, is a public, unqualified, and unambiguous declaration of war**...This therefore is not merely the case of an injury to be repaired, but of the public safety to be secured against the present and future designs of an irreconcilable, desperate, and treacherous enemy. **Against an enemy of this description no effectual security can be obtained, otherwise than by such a reduction of his power, as shall not only defeat his actual preparations, but establish a permanent restraint upon his future means of offence**. (Emphasis added)

Despite this, Mornington made an offer of peace to Tipu. He wrote a letter to Tipu informing him that he would send Major Doveton for talks. Tipu simply ignored the letter. Mornington then wrote a *second* letter seeking a response from Tipu for the first letter. In November 1798, Tipu wrote back accusing the Governor General of trying to "meditate hostilities" and bluntly told him that he had discredited Mornington's first letter. Between November 1798 and January 1799, Mornington kept writing to Tipu urging him to talk peace with Major Doveton. As before, Tipu yet again assumed that the British were scared of his renewing power what with his overtures to the French and the Muslim kings abroad. As a consequence, he didn't take any of Mornington's letters seriously. The British patience was wearing thin but Tipu's 13 February 1799 letter was the final straw:

Being frequently disposed to make excursions and hunt, I am accordingly proceeding upon a hunting expedition. You will be pleased to send Major Doveton [about whom you had repeatedly written]...Always continue to gratify me by friendly letters.

Tipu had to pay the ultimate price for this insolence.

Mornington's conclusions about Tipu in his Minute had proven to be perfectly accurate. He had already readied his troops for an eventual war even as he continued to make peace offers to Tipu in the hope that sense would prevail upon him. On 14 December 1798, Mornington had issued an order instructing all the area commanders in South India to prepare for a war with Tipu. The Board of Directors of the East India Company in England approved a sum of Five Crore Rupees for "prosecuting Tipu."

British Declaration of war

And so on 22 February 1799, Mornington issued a "Declaration" on behalf of the East India Company and its allies, the Nizam and the Marathas. The Declaration listed the various violations of the 1792 Treaty that Tipu had committed—including his courting of the French and other foreign powers. It ended by saying that the British and their allies were still "anxious to effect a friendly arrangement with the Sultan...and concert a treaty on such conditions as would lead to the establishment of a secure and permanent peace." A letter on those lines was despatched to Tipu. Nothing came out of it.

It appeared as if Tipu had resolved to walk into the arms of disaster with his eyes open. And he had nothing going for him. His army had by then further dwindled down: a paltry 33,000 infantry and 15,000 cavalry. It was a weak and ineffective force by all counts. For a full year, only two months' of pay had been distributed and the soldiers were enfeebled thanks to insufficient food and nutrition, which in turn was the consequence of a near-bankrupt treasury. The danger of deserters on the battlefield also loomed large. The only area he was strong in was artillery.

On 11 February 1799, the allied army contingents began to march towards Srirangapattana from various locations—from Vellore, Bombay, and Hyderabad. Apart from just *one* minor setback from which it soon recovered, the allied forces defeated Tipu's army in every single battle. This was compounded by Tipu's ill-conceived strategy, which actually helped the British reach his very doorstep. Here is how Lewin Bowring describes this costly gaffe of Tipu:

The mistake of Tipu in supposing that the British army would take the direct road from Bangalore to [Srirangapattana], and attack that place from the north, as Lord Cornwallis had done in 1792, was of immense service to Lord Harris. Under this anticipation, Tipu had ordered the destruction of all forage on the more direct route, which he held in force. But the English general, by marching to the south and crossing the Kaveri at Sosile', not only found ample fodder, but effected the passage of the ford without opposition. He was now within fifteen miles of Seringapatam, and Tipu found out that all his efforts to prevent the enemy from reaching within striking distance of his capital had been completely frustrated.

The Storming of Srirangapattana

Tipu really had no chance. In just two months—February to April—Tipu was reduced to fighting a desperate battle for his own personal, *physical* survival. On 3 April 1799 the allied army had encamped barely a few miles on the southwest of the Srirangapattana fort.

On 7 April, General Harris successfully laid siege to Tipu Sultan's fort. The so-called Tiger of Mysore was yet again a prisoner in his own house. And as in the previous instance, he called for peace terms instead of putting up a gallant defence. General Harris' reply was straightforward: he simply reminded Tipu of his insolent letter to Mornington. On 14 April, the Bombay contingent arrived at Srirangapattana.

The pounding of his fort began. Initially, the allied attack was met with strong resistance by the Frenchmen in Tipu's army but they proved no match in terms of numbers or strategic advantage. Indeed, the total number of Frenchmen serving at the time in Tipu's army was a paltry 120.

On 20 April, Tipu again sued for peace. General Harris agreed and laid down his conditions:

1. Dismiss all the Frenchmen in Tipu's service.
2. Cede half of Tipu's territories to the allies.
3. Pay 2 million Sterling: half immediately and the remainder in six months.
4. Release all prisoners.
5. Send the eldest two sons of Tipu as hostages.
6. Send four chief officers too, as hostages.

General Harris gave 24 hours to Tipu to agree to these terms. Tipu didn't respond.

By 24 April, resistance on the western side of Tipu's fort broke down. The north-west bastion was dismantled and only a few guns remained on the southern side of the fort. By 27 April, Tipu's troops occupying the trenches of the fort were successfully beaten back and the allied army advanced proportionately.

On 28 April, Tipu submitted another offer of peace. This time, he agreed to send ambassadors for talks. However, he received the same reply: there would be no change in the terms that were laid down by General Harris. Tipu's last attempt had failed. He took out his frustration by killing 13 British prisoners most horribly—their necks were twisted by professional wrestlers (*Jettis*).

On 2 May, the allied guns and cannons unrelentingly battered the Western side of fort until a massive breach was accomplished. Orders were then issued "for an assault at 1 P.M. on the 4th."

Tipu's last day

On 4 May 1799, Tipu woke up early, inspected his fort minutely, bathed, and made offerings of money and clothes to the poor. He also gave a caparisoned elephant to a priest and distributed a bag of oilseeds, oxen, and money to some Brahmins. He had turned to God to save him from impending doom, something that Bowring describes as follows:

Tipu, a prey to despair in the imminent peril which threatened him, condescended, in spite of his orthodox Islamism, to have recourse to the prayers and incantations of the Brahmans whom he had hitherto invariably despised and ill-treated.

A short while after this, he received news that Sayyad Ghafur, his trusted officer had died heroically.

The allied troops had entered the fort with relative ease and overcame opposition with equal ease. Before afternoon, the British flag was hoisted on the ramparts of Tipu's fort. Tipu now charged forward, motivating his men to give a determined battle. However, it was a little too late in the day. The allied troops had already seized decisive advantage.

Even worse, Tipu's own soldiers deserted him, forcing him to retreat. Even that wasn't easy. He received a bullet wound on his breast and a second one on the right side when his horse fell down. He was then placed in a palanquin but even that proved useless because he soon encountered some British soldiers. Tipu's end came swiftly. We can turn to Bowring again:

Soon afterwards some European soldiers entered the gateway, one of whom attempted to take off his richly-jewelled sword-belt, when Tipu, sorely wounded as he was, made a cut at the man, and wounded him in the knee. The enraged soldier levelled his musket and shot him in the head, causing instantaneous death.

The British had taken over pretty much the entire fort even as the soldier shot Tipu. General Baird, who had led the charge inside the fort, sent for Major Allan to find out what had happened to Tipu. Here is Major Allan's eyewitness account of the episode:

The Death of Tipu Sultan

Later that evening, and with torch in hands, a search was conducted for Tipu or for his body....His body was finally recovered; it had four wounds, therein the body and one in the temple...Tipu's horse was found shot, and then his palanquin, beneath which a slave *had concealed himself...the slave pointed out his master's body... [Tipu's] coarse dark face was fixed in its last expression of fury and despair, and there was a bullet through his head—fired...by a common soldier who coveted his jewelled sword-belt.*

This was how the "Tiger" of Mysore, Tipu Sultan met his maker and took with him his ambitious dream of waging a jihad on the Indian soil.

However, the British did not usurp the throne of Mysore. Instead, they handed it over to the rightful descendants of the original rulers, the Wodeyars.

24 June 1799

We shall at all times consider ourselves as under your protection and orders. Your having established us must ever be fresh in the memory of our posterity, from one generation to the other. Our off-spring can never forget the attachment to your Government on whose support we shall depend. Sd—

Lakshmi Ammanni & Devaji Ammanni

Tipu's Place of Death as seen today

This letter mentioned at the beginning of this book was written to the British by the respective widows of Chikka Krishnaraja Wodeyar and Chamaraja Wodeyar after Tipu's death. Peace was restored to the Mysore kingdom and its citizens were finally freed from the yoke of royal exploitation and torment.

At the end of this sordid saga, we cannot help but ask an obvious question: wouldn't it have been better if the British had killed Tipu during the Third Anglo-Mysore war and restored the kingdom to the Wodeyars? After all, the story of Tipu begins with Hyder Ali, a common soldier who betrayed and snatched the kingdom from its legitimate rulers. His son then emerged as an unparalleled tyrant and a savage Islamic bigot who inflicted untold atrocities upon Hindus and plotted to share India with the French and alien Muslim kings.

How do the British, who restored Mysore to its legitimate rulers, become traitors?

Now the question again: *was Tipu's struggle a struggle for India's Independence and was he a freedom fighter?*

19

The True Legacy of Tipu

Whether a person can be called a freedom fighter or no will be clear when we examine the historical timeline. After Ashoka's death, the whole of India was never united under a single empire. Indeed, until the 1857 war, there was no concept of India as a single, politically-unified nation. Various kings used to fight one another to either defend themselves or extend their territories. The Nawab of Arcot and the Nairs of the Malabar fought against Tipu in the same way as Tipu fought against the Marathas and the Kodavas. The Marathas hated the Hyder-Tipu duo as much as the latter hated the British.

The Marathas who had invited Hyder Ali to fight against the British as early as 1771 hated the British with greater intensity. But then, the same Marathas allied with the British in the Third and Fourth Anglo-Mysore wars. And it's not just that. The Mughals fought against the Rajputs, and the Marathas fought against the Mughals. And thus, until all of these Indian kings lost their kingdoms one after the other, and until the British took over most of India, there was no common enemy.

However, by 1857, all kings, feudatories, Sultans, Nizams, Nawabs, and other royal dynasties had been completely subjugated by the British, who then emerged as the common enemy. Apart from Ashoka, the only other king who had—barring a few regions—the whole of India under his control was Akbar. The British were the only empire who managed to surpass both Ashoka and Akbar in this respect. Therefore, it was only after this common enemy emerged that the people of India started a movement to reclaim their country. This phenomenon can reasonably be defined as a freedom struggle in the sense in which we understand it today.

The British tried to give a name to the war of 1857 by calling it the Sepoy Mutiny. It was also known as the Indian Mutiny. Vinayak Damodar Savarkar—or Veer Savarkar—who wrote the "The History of the War of Indian Independence," termed the Sepoy Mutiny as the First War of Independence, a phrase that came into widespread usage. However, the Sikhs were unhappy with this terminology. They insisted that the First Anglo-Sikh war of 1845-56 be called the First War of Independence.

What does all this indicate?

The wars and conflicts prior to the 1857 war do not come under the ambit of the definition of the term "freedom struggle." Therefore, none of the people who fought in them can be called freedom fighters. They were just conflicts and battles fought to defend and preserve specific territories. Aren't our literary and academic eminences aware of this simple truth? How does Tipu Sultan, who fought against the British, Marathas, Kodavas, Nairs, et al to either defend his territory or to conquer that of other kings, become a freedom fighter? In which case, why can't we call Siraj-ud-Daula a freedom fighter? After all, he fought in 1757 in the Battle of Plassey against the British. If the act of Tipu Sultan taking French help to drive the British out of India is termed as freedom struggle, how is it different from that of Siraj-ud-Daula who also took French help 25 years prior to Tipu? By this token, doesn't Tipu's own father, Hyder Ali who fought the British also become a freedom fighter? How can one fight for the freedom of a country at a time when there was no concept of a single nation-state and a single, united Government?

Also, can we call the Raja of Travancore, the Marathas, and the Nizam of Hyderabad as traitors because they took the help of the British to fight Tipu's atrocities? The Nizam of Hyderabad sent a contingent of 10 Battalions in the Fourth Anglo-Mysore in which Tipu was killed. This force included 3600 French soldiers. And we've seen the close relationship that Tipu had with the French. How do we explain this using the Tipu-as-freedom-fighter logic?

In spite of this, if one continues to insist that Tipu was a freedom fighter, another question arises: what part of his freedom struggle compelled him to wage wanton wars and unleash unprovoked aggression against the hapless Hindus in the Malabar and Coorg? What part of his freedom struggle compelled him to commit genocide against those Hindus and/or convert them en masse? Indeed, the British hardly had a presence in those regions.

It is eminently clear, from whatever angle one looks at it, that there is simply no way one can conclude that Tipu's fight against the British constitutes a struggle for freedom.

Indeed, Tipu was anything but a freedom fighter. He was neither an able administrator nor was he interested in the welfare of his subjects. Like every territory-hungry tyrant, he had grand designs to conquer all of India, an ambition that was fuelled by his extreme religious fanaticism. He had no regard for the soil of India, and not an ounce of respect for its culture. His allegiance lay first and last to his religion. The verse inscribed on his epitaph at Srirangapattana provides eminent testimony to this fact. It commemorates him as the "Haidari Sultan who died for the Faith." The text in the Farsi original and its translation (emphasized) follow:

Noor Islam wa din z' dunya raft
The light of Islam and the faith left the world;
Tipu ba wajah din Muhammad shahid shud
Tipu on account of the faith of Muhammad was a martyr
Shamshe'r gum shud
The sword was lost
Nasal Haidar shahid akbar shud
The offspring of Haidar was a great martyr

The verse was composed by Mir Hussein Ali and written by Abdul Kadir. The date inscribed on the tomb is 1213 Hijri which corresponds to the year 1799. Lewin B. Bowring who has provided the translation remarks that "[d] uring the perilous days of the Mutiny, it is said that bigoted Musalmans congregated at this spot to say their prayers and breathe secret aspirations for the re-ascendancy of their faith." This statement needs no further explanation as to what Tipu really stood for.

Indeed, the true legacy of Tipu lies in his character, mental makeup, and deeds over 17 years.

Tipu considered himself as the protector and propagator of Islam. In his fanaticism-fuelled worldview, people of other faiths were sinners filled with ignorance of false faiths. According to Tipu, Islam was the only true faith and everybody who didn't follow the Prophet and his teachings were kaffirs and traitors. He called his kingdom the *Khudadaad Sarkar*, or the Kingdom Given by God. He labored under the belief that his wars against Hindu kings and the British were Holy Wars (Jihad) aimed at establishing and extending the Only True Faith.

If we look back at history, we find that Tipu wasn't an exception. He had a fanatical precedence—Muhammad Ghaznavid, Muhammad Ghori, Muhammad Tughlaq, the Bahamani Sultans and the Mughals to name just a few prominent fanatical Muslim invaders and rulers.

Islam and Christianity are religions alien to India. The first Islamic invasion occurred in Sindh in the year 711. The combined forces of the Gurjaras, Pratiharas and Rajputs decisively repelled the Arab invasion in the Battle of Rajasthan fought in 738 C.E. However, the brutal chapter of the Islamic invasion and conquest of India opened in the 11th Century. In 1001 C.E. the Afghan ruler Muhammad Ghaznavid attacked and subdued Jayapala, the king of the Shahi dynasty. From then on, he invaded India 17 times leaving a trail of destruction and pillage every single time. It was Muhammad Ghori's turn next. He began his invasion in 1191 C.E. at the Battle of Tarain where he was roundly defeated by Prithviraj Chauhan. However, Prithviraj Chauhan committed the cardinal blunder of sparing his life. The very next year, Ghori attacked India yet again. This time, the nation had to pay a hugely expensive price that was extracted over several centuries. The last vestiges of the nearly-1000 year long Muslim rule in India were finally wiped out in 1948 by the Indian army which unseated the Nizam of Hyderabad.

If the Dutch, the French, the British, and the Portuguese came to India for engaging in trade in spices, the Ghaznis and the Ghoris came for the express purpose of plunder and conversion. Whatever the purpose, the end result was the same: the victimization, impoverishment, and enslavement of Hindus. If the Muslims tried to achieve this by force and brutality, the Missionaries, who accompanied the British, the French, the Dutch, and the Portuguese, tried to do the same through covert means.

Tipu's legacy is therefore, simply a continuation of this long-drawn and brutal legacy of Muslim rule in India. It is pertinent to quote Will Durant's oft-quoted but prescient summary of the Islamic conquest of India:

The Islamic conquest of India is probably the bloodiest story in history. It is a discouraging tale, for its evident moral is that civilization is a precious good, whose delicate complex of order and freedom, culture and peace, can at any moment be overthrown by barbarians invading from without or multiplying within.

Equally, Tipu does not become a champion of the Kannada language merely because he was born in Devanahalli. If that were true, he wouldn't have forcibly replaced Kannada with Farsi in his administration. Nor does he become a national hero because he was born in India. If this were true, he wouldn't have invited Zaman Shah, the Persian King and the Caliph to invade India.

As we have seen, whenever Tipu subdued any king, he would not only loot the king but would also convert the king and his subjects. He would also carry away the womenfolk and rape them and then add them to his Zanaanaa (harem). However, the British exhibited far more dignity in their dealings with Tipu than Tipu did in his behavior with vanquished kings. Our secular and Marxist historians in their zeal to paint Tipu as an unblemished hero conveniently paint the British as heartless murderers. However, the truth is the exact opposite. After Tipu's death in 1799, the British transported his royal family to the safety of the Vellore fort and treated them with the courtesy that befits royalty. When the British captured Srirangapattana, they found that his Zanaanaa contained over 650 women. And the number of staff comprising servants, eunuchs, and guards required to support this massive harem brought the total up to more than a thousand people.

Tipu had kept Hyder Ali's family separate. Hyder's Zananaa contained more than 200 women which included his wives and concubines and the wives and concubines of Hyder's other sons not to mention the equally large support staff. Tipu used to pay a monthly allowance of One Lakh Pagodas for the maintenance of his father's women and children. After Tipu's death, the British increased this maintenance money and paid it out of their own pockets.

```
                    ┌──────────────────────┐
                    │      HYDER ALI       │
                    └──────────────────────┘
        ┌─────────────────┘            └─────────────────┐
        ▼                                                ▼
┌──────────────────────────────┐        ┌──────────────────────────┐
│ Fateh Ali Khan (TIPU SULTAN) │        │     KARIM SHAH           │
└──────────────────────────────┘        │    (Safdar Shikhoh)      │
                                         └──────────────────────────┘
```

- Fateh Hyder : 7 Sons, 6 Daughters
- Abdul Khalik : 2 Sons
- Mohi-uddin: 5 Sons, 2 Daughters
- Moiz-uddin: 1 Son, 3 Daughters
- Muhammad Subhan: 5 Sons 6 Daughters
- Shukar Ullah: 6 Sons, 4 Daughters
- Sarwar-uddin: 2 Daughters
- Jamal-uddin: 1 Son
- Munir-uddin: 1 Son, 2 Daughters
- Muhammad Sultan : 3 Sons, 3 Daughters
- Ahmad Sultan: 3 Daughters

- Ghulam Ali: 3 Sons, 1 Daughters
- Imam Baksh: 1 Son

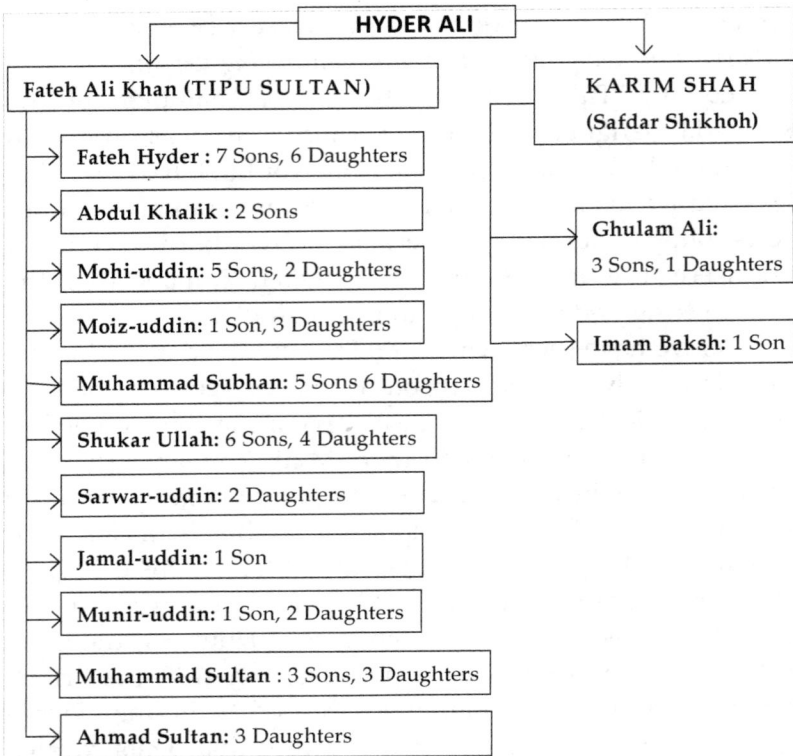

According to one estimate, Hyder Ali had a total of 89 great grandchildren.

The behavior and conduct of Tipu's sons at Vellore was venal. They were prisoners for all purposes but lived a lavish life thanks solely to British generosity. With no work to do, they began indulging in treachery and plotting. They instigated other Muslim prisoners at the Vellore fort to rise up in mutiny, which was swiftly put down by the British. They were then shifted to the British fort at Calcutta. Even in aftermath of this rebellion, the British did not stop their royal pension. Over time, the members of Tipu's family—who had multiplied to about a thousand now—became part of the teeming millions of Calcutta. Some left for Pakistan a few years before the Partition. One of the great granddaughters of Tipu, a fabled beauty named Noor Inayath Khan worked as a spy on the British side in World War II against the Germans and earned international renown.

SHRABANI BASU

SPY PRINCESS

THE LIFE OF
NOOR
INAYAT
KHAN

PREFACE BY PIR ZIA INAYAT-KHAN

*Noor Inayat Khan
- Tipu's Descendant*

The people of the Mysore region fondly, reverentially recall the legacy of the Wodeyars and the Diwans who worked under them. It was the untiring efforts of these Diwans that eventually made Mysore a Model State. Hyder Ali is remembered as a usurper while Tipu is remembered as a cruel tyrant who wreaked havoc on not just kings but on his own citizens. Besides, what was the father-son duo's exact contribution to Mysore and Srirangapattana? We have examined the true nature of their "contribution" so far in this book.

The capital of the Mysore kingdom was shifted from Mysore city to Srirangapattana in 1610 C.E. by Raja Wodeyar, who ruled from 1578-1617. Raja Wodeyar recognized the strategic importance of Srirangapattana which is an island by the River Cauvery. It provided a natural defence against enemies. It was Raja Wodeyar who truly built Srirangapattana and made it a vibrant centre of culture, and not the usurper Hyder Ali and his son, who converted it into a massive den of despotism. But for the father-son duo, Srirangapattana would've risen in stature to that of Mysore today—as a centre of refined culture and a hub of high learning.

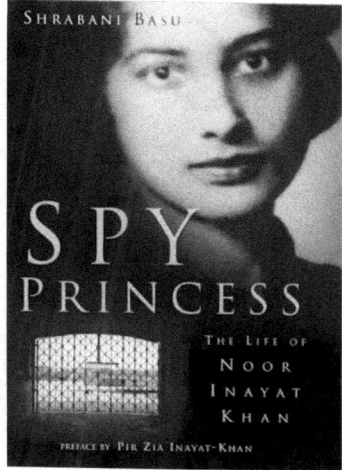

20

The Tiger of Mysore?

Tipu Sultan as the "Tiger" of Mysore is perhaps one of the more enduring myths in circulation not just in Karnataka but throughout the country. "Mysoreina Huli," "Sher-e-Mysore" and similar vernacular equivalents have been current for more than 60 years. It's a truism that several famous myths are perchance woven around at least a grain of truth. However, did Tipu really qualify to be called the Tiger of Mysore?

This myth is derived from local legend, which in turn was derived from illiterate bards who sang Tipu's praises in the hope of earning a few coins. The myth holds that Tipu earned this title after killing a tiger with his bare hands. However, Sunad Raghuram has convincingly demonstrated that Tipu did no such thing in an article entitled *"Did the Tiger of Mysore really tame a tiger?"* But then it's also a truism that myths are easy to create but enormously tough to break.

The political dispensation and discourse in India since 1947 has ensured that it is rewarding to keep such myths in circulation. Bhagwan S Gidwani's phony historical fiction, *The Sword of Tipu Sultan* is perhaps the most celebrated accomplishment in furthering this myth. That novel was a work aimed at appeasing the political current of the day, and not a historical novel faithful to the facts of history. These facts, as we have seen, are entirely different.

It bears repeating that *Tipu never took the British head-on in any battle*. The British did their homework on Tipu with great patience and care, over several months. They exercised immense restraint despite Tipu's recalcitrant behavior and his wanton violation of various treaties. If Tipu indeed was the tiger that he's made out to be, he wouldn't have surrendered meekly after the British allies captured the Bangalore fort in 1791. If he was indeed the tiger, he would've rather sacrificed his life protecting his young sons instead of giving them away as hostages.

Even if we disregard all these facts, the key question remains: what exactly were Tipu's contributions to the Mysore State? Were they the palaces he built so that he could satisfy his whims and indulgences? Were they the armouries that he used for launching unprovoked attacks on neighbours and hapless citizens? There's also no dearth of Marxist historians who claim that he was the first to "innovate" rocket technology in India while carefully concealing the fact that this "rocket technology" was given by the French to Tipu.

In January 2010 in a seminar entitled *Life and Achievements of Tipu Sultan* held in Mysore, the legislator Tanveer Sait commanded thus: "The Government must throw more light on the contributions of Tipu Sultan towards modernizing Mysore." The retired Vice Chancellor, Professor Sheik Ali said in the same seminar, "Tipu possessed the foresight and the goal of liberating this country from foreign forces and steer it on a path of development." However, Tanveer Sait didn't mention Tipu's contributions to the Mysore state; nor did the Vice Chancellor elucidate Tipu's foresight or his goals. The reason: there was nothing to say in either case. What was Tipu's rule except a dark chapter of atrocity? If we observe most people who praise Tipu, we find that they exhibit immense rhetorical fervor but are woefully devoid of facts. We need to ask these Tipu-worshippers to show us

A Famous Painting Depicting Tipu as the Tiger of Mysore

exactly *one* example of a positive contribution that this father-son duo made in their 40-year long rule. Just one example on the lines of Krishnaraja Wodeyar IV and his diwan, Sir M. Visveshwarayya.

Perhaps the most succinct and accurate assessement of Tipu's character is given by G.A Henty in the preface of his *The Tiger of Mysore:*

Tippoo...reveled in acts of the most abominable cruelty. It would seem that he massacred for the very pleasure of massacring, and hundreds of British captives were killed by famine, poison, or torture, simply to gratify his lust for murder. Patience was shown towards this monster until patience became a fault, and our inaction was naturally ascribed by him to fear.

• • •

Timeline of
Tipu Sultan's Regime and Life

Timeline	Event
1609	Raja Wodeyar, feudatory of the Vijayanagar Empire declares independence and founds the Wodeyar Dynasty at Mysore.
1736	Chikka Krishnaraja Wodeyar is crowned the king of a weakened Wodeyar dynasty.
1721	Hyder Ali is born.
1749	Heads a small contingent on behalf of the Mysore army in support of Nasir Jung. Loots Nasir Jung's treasure after his murder.
1751	Participates in the siege of Tiruchinapalli, an early milestone in his career.
1753	Fateh Ali Khan, more famously known as Tipu Sultan is born at Devanahalli near Bangalore.
1755	Hyder Ali promoted as the *Faujdaar* (Commander) of Dindigul.
1757	Saves total destruction of Mysore from the Marathas. Decorated with the *Fateh Hyder Bahadur* title.
1761	Usurps the throne of Mysore and declares himself the Nawab.
1769	Tipu flogged publicly on the orders of Hyder Ali for desertion and cowardice on the battlefield.
1782	• Victory against British Colonel Braithwaite. First major military milestone in his career. • Hyder Ali succumbs to a terminal illness of the back at Narasingarayanapet.
1782-83	Tipu crowned as the Nawab of Mysore.

1784	• War with British at Mangalore ends with British defeat. Treaty of Mangalore signed. Major victory for Tipu. • Captures Raichur from Nizam Ali Khan. Wrests control of territory between Tungabhadra and Krishna rivers.
1785	Raids Coorg and Adoni.
1786	• Raids and captures Periyapattana, Belur, Manjarabad (Sakaleshpur), and Badami. • Declares himself the *Padshah*
1787	• Captures Bijapur, Ahmednagar, Anegondi, Savanur, Rayadurga and Harapanahalli. • Issues a decree prohibiting the manufacture and sale of alcohol in his dominions.
1788	• Raids Coorg a second time and ravages it resulting in large scale death, and destruction of temples and property. • Raids Calicut (Kozhikode) and razes it to the ground.
1789	• Attacks the Travancore Raja. Repelled once. Is victorious the second time. Travancore ravaged. Is defeated the third time. • Lord Cornwallis is appointed the British East India Company's Governor General of India.
1790	Cornwallis enters into a treaty with the Marathas, and the Nizam against Tipu. Grand Army of allies formed.
1791	• The Grand Army attacks and wrests Bangalore from Tipu. • More successes for the allied forces as other important territories are wrested from Tipu.

1792	• The Grand Army captures more than three-fourths of Tipu's dominions.
	• Third Anglo-Mysore war begins. Tipu is isolated inside his own fort at Srirangapattana.
	• Tipu surrenders and signs a humiliating treaty with the Allied forces.
1796	• Tipu makes overtures to the French to avenge his humiliation. Several agreements are concluded.
	• Tipu courts the Afghan ruler Zaman Shah to launch a Jihad in India.
1797	• Tipu formalises a plan with Zaman Shah for a military expedition.
1798	• Napoleon Bonaparte replies to Tipu's letters favourably.
	• Tipu courts the Caliph with appeals to invade India and wipe out the British.
	• Tipu is warned by British Governor General Lord Mornington against allying with the French.
1799	• Tipu is rebuffed by the Caliph who is a friend of the British.
	• Lord Mornington declares war against Tipu.
	• Tipu is killed by a British soldier on 4 May inside his Srirangapattana fort.
	• Mysore kingdom restored to the Wodeyars by the British.

Bibliography

1. *Hyder Ali and Tipu Sultan* – Lewin B. Bowring
2. *History of Kerala (Vol 1 and 2)*—Padmanabha Menon
3. *Mysore Gazetteer (Vol 1 and 2)*—Lewis Rice
4. *Mysore Gazetteer (Vol 1 and 2)*—Hayavadana Rao
5. *Mysore and Coorg*—Lewis Rice
6. *Selected Letters of Tipu Sultan*—Colonel William Kirkpatrick
7. *Nishan-i-Haidari*—Mir Hussein Ali Kirmani, translated by Colonel William Miles
8. *Tipu Sultan's Mysore: An Economic Study*—M.H. Gopal
9. *Tipu Sultan X'Rayed*—I.M. Muthanna
10. *History of Sanskrit Literature in Kerala*—Vatakkankoor Raja Raja Varma
11. *Malabar Manual*—William Logan
12. *Study of Tipu Sultan*—Colonel Palsokar
13. *Tipu Sultan: Villain or Hero?*—Various authors, Voice of India
14. *Life of Tipu Sultan*—Pakistan Administrative Staff College, Lahore, translated by Bernard Wycliffe
15. *Madras Gazette and Courier*—1791 to 1799
16. *Calcutta Gazette and Courier*—1789 to 1801
17. *The Tiger of Mysore: A Story of the war with Tippoo Sahib*—G.A. Henty

END

Index

CPSIA information can be obtained
at www.ICGtesting.com
Printed in the USA
LVHW050142151221
706185LV00022B/2686

9 788192 788463